TRAINING TO IMAGINE

# Training to
# IMAGINE

## Practical Improvisational Theatre Techniques for Trainers and Managers to Enhance Creativity, Teamwork, Leadership, and Learning

## Kat Koppett

FOREWORD TO FIRST EDITION BY
## Sivasailam "Thiagi" Thiagarajan

FOREWORD TO SECOND EDITION BY
## Joel Goodman

SECOND EDITION

STERLING, VIRGINIA

Sty/us

Published by Stylus Publishing, LLC
22883 Quicksilver Drive
Sterling, Virginia 20166-2102

Library of Congress Cataloging-in-Publication Data
Koppett, Kat, 1965–
   Training to imagine : practical improvisational
theatre techniques for trainers and managers to
enhance creativity, teamwork, leadership and
learning / Kat Koppett ; foreword by Sivasailam
"Thiagi" Thiagarajan.—2nd ed.
   p.  cm.
Includes bibliographical references and index.
ISBN 978-1-57922-591-9 (cloth : alk. paper)
ISBN 978-1-57922-592-6 (pbk. : alk. paper)
ISBN 978-1-57922-593-3 (library networkable
e-edition)
ISBN 978-1-57922-594-0 (consumer e-edition)
1. Employees—Training of.   2. Training.
3. Improvisation (Acting)   I. Title.
HF5549.5.T7K658   2013
658.3'124—dc23                          2012010150

13-digit ISBN: 978-1-57922-591-9 (cloth)
13-digit ISBN: 978-1-57922-592-6 (paper)
13-digit ISBN: 978-1-57922-593-3 (library
networkable e-edition)
13-digit ISBN: 978-1-57922-594-0 (consumer
e-edition)

Printed in the United States of America

All first editions printed on acid-free paper
that meets the American National Standards Institute
Z39-48 Standard.

Bulk Purchases

Quantity discounts are available for use in
workshops and for staff development.
Call 1-800-232-0223

Second Edition, 2013

*For Lia*

*My favorite improvisational
playmate and teacher*

# CONTENTS

## APPENDIX

The list of people and organizations to whom I am indebted for the knowledge and experiences reflected in this text continues to grow. It includes:

The companies I have been privileged to perform with and learn from: Freestyle Repertory Theatre, BATS Improv, Chicago City Limits, Unexpected Company, and my current performing family, The Mop & Bucket Company (www.mopco.org).

Alain Rostain of Creative Advantage, who gave me my first full-time professional opportunity and was a pioneer in recognizing the value of improv in the business setting.

The members of Applied Improv Network (AIN), founded by Alain Rostain and Paul Z. Jackson, which has become home to thousands of applied improv practitioners around the world. The knowledge, wisdom, skills, and mind-sets that I have been exposed to there are of incomparable value. Collectively, that community continues to build a thriving, growing field, which is having a stronger impact on our world than anyone yet realizes. AIN members give me hope for the future and I thank them deeply for all of their "stuff" that is reflected here.

The folks of Performance of a Lifetime—Cathy Salit, Maureen Kelly, David Nackman—who consistently move my work, and the work of the field, to higher and deeper levels. I am profoundly grateful for their generous collaborations and for introducing me to a number of my most cherished colleagues.

My professional mentors, colleagues, and friends—among a very many more—Sivasailam "Thiagi" Thiagarajan, grandfather and mentor to us all, Andy Kimball of Qube Learning, Rebecca Stockley,

William Hall, Rich Cox, Dan Klein, Patricia Ryan Madsen, Kenn Adams, Laura Livingston, Matthew Richter, Kevin Eikenberry, Elizabeth Doty, Kimberly Mohne Hill, Cal Sutliff, Adam Grupper, Sevanne Kessarjian, Shannon Polly, Michael Rock, Geoff Tarson, Dion Flynn, and Zohar Adner.

John von Knorring, my publisher, who again said "yes" to working on this book and whose insightful, firm, and kind comments have resulted in a text I believe justifies this second edition. Additional thanks to production editor, Alexandra Hartnett; copyeditor, Linda Carlson; and proofreader, Sue Boshers, for their conscientious and supportive editing.

And of course, my wonderful husband and partner, Michael Burns, with whom I get to improvise at home and at work in the most delightful ways every day of our lives. How did that happen?

My colleague Kat Koppett has completed a courageous and conscientious job in writing this book. It is a pleasure for me to write a foreword to it.

I am an instructional designer and management trainer. My academic friends take great delight in pointing out that instructional design and improv games are totally incompatible. Effective instruction, they tell me, is based on removing variance and prepackaging activities to make them replicable. The focus is on the "need-to-know" content that directly contributes to the achievement of pre-specified and measurable objectives and the avoidance of nice-and-fluffy activities. I learned a lot about the importance of instructional analysis, structure, and control in my PhD program. But what I currently use in my training design and delivery comes from what I learned as a street-corner magician.

In this book, Kat brings a new perspective to the training and management scene. She provides practical guidance to trainers and managers who have become aware that the complex chaos in today's workplace requires something different from the standard, systematic, rational approach. Many scholars are now offering conceptual frameworks that incorporate improvisation into management science and instructional design. Rather than writing another such academic tome, Kat provides a practical sourcebook. I can provide empirical justification for Kat's approach from my background in cognitive sciences. But I'd rather tell you a few stories.

Every summer, my wife and I return to Chennai, India (which used to be called Madras), where I spent the first 30 years of my life. Summer is not the best time of the year to be in the sweltering heat of Chennai, but that is when my wife (who teaches school) gets her vacation. We spend the month visiting family and doing some bleeding-heart liberal community work in a school where we taught and in a village where my grandfather founded an orphanage.

In 1999, however, I decided to do something different and undertake a longitudinal ethnographic study of instructional effectiveness. In other words, I wanted to track down the ex-students from my days as a high school science and math teacher and interview them. To keep things simple, I whittled down my interview protocol to just two open-ended questions:

- What do you remember about my days as a teacher?

- What is the most useful thing that you learned from me?

The results were depressing. Several of my students are dead from a variety of diseases and accidents. I could not track down some of my favorite students. A few of the students whom I interviewed did not even remember me. And none of them could recall the things that I taught, such as the proof for the Pythagorean theorem or the statement of the principle of Archimedes.

The results were also exciting. Apparently, I had a significant impact on the lives of a few students.

Here are the stories from two girls in my class. Both of them have grown up to be forty-something, happy homemakers:

Suseela's daughter is in college now. I had heard some rumors that this bright Brahmin girl had eloped with a lower-caste bus conductor.

> What do I remember about you? We were in an all-girls class-room, and you told us stories. You were supposed to teach the Moral Instruction class period every Monday morning, but you kept telling us romantic stories about Laila and Majnu, Akbar's son and Anarkali, and other star-crossed lovers. You know what was the most important thing that you taught me? I don't have to be like those tragic heroines. If my parents or my community doesn't want me to marry somebody I loved, I'd go ahead and marry him anyhow.

Vasantha was from the same classroom. She is now married to an affluent shopkeeper and often works in the showroom.

You know what I remember? Your look of calm defiance. Remember the day my mother stormed into your classroom during your chemistry demonstration? She started yelling at you for not maintaining discipline in the classroom. She was upset because I had gone to a movie the night before with my girlfriend Banu. I did not tell her about it until she caught me sneaking back home. My mother accused you of encouraging low-caste girls to spoil her daughter. And then she seized a beaker from your table and threw it against the wall. She left the room in a great rage as the glass shattered. We were all shocked and embarrassed, but you did not say anything. You just picked up the pieces of glass and put them in the sink. Then you filled another beaker with a solution of potassium permanganate and continued talking about diffusion. You know what you taught me? Most grown-ups are frauds. My mother may have an expensive statue of Gandhi in her pooja room with her idols of Shiva. But she has no clue about what Gandhi meant when he said that we should respect people from other castes and other religions.

Here are the stories from three of the boys I interviewed.

I remember Kandan as a student from a family of five siblings in the slums. His father worked as a peon in a local bank. Kandan is now working as a clerk in the same bank. He has three sons and makes enough money to lead a fairly comfortable life.

What do I remember about you as a teacher? I remember the day you came to the police station during lunchtime when they arrested me for vandalism. I remember your pleading on my behalf with the police inspector. You told him things about my having a great potential. The policeman kept trying to convince you that I am just a juvenile delinquent from the slums, but you personally guaranteed that I won't get into trouble again. Not only did you spring me from the police station, but you did not tell anything to my father. What did you teach me? I remember how to solve simultaneous equations in algebra. That's what you taught us the day I came back from the police station. You told us that it would be useful in my future life, and I believed you. Actually, the only time I use it is when I want to impress my boys with my ability to solve puzzles.

Nadhan has taken over his father's construction business. He has made a pile of money doing government contracts. He insists on standing respectfully as I sit on a comfortable couch in his air-conditioned office.

What do I remember? The class on the water cycle, which you taught us on the Inspection Day. Even now I can make a rain gauge and measure how many centimeters of rain fell overnight.

With some prompting from Nadhan I remembered the incident. All teachers spent a couple of weeks preparing elaborate lesson plans for the Inspection Day, during which the District Educational Officer (DEO) visits classrooms, observes teachers, and writes evaluation reports. This event is a big deal because future school funding depends on the inspection report. But I did not spend any time preparing my lessons, because I was in a romantic haze during those days, and I believed that the DEO would probably skip my classroom because he had only a limited period of time. It was a dark and stormy afternoon, with the monsoon rain pouring down. The DEO walked into the back of the room while I was getting ready to teach about the preparation of chlorine. But I changed my mind at the last moment. A part of the thatch roof in the front of the classroom had blown away, and the rain was pouring down through the big gaping hole. I decided to make hay while the sun was not shining and deliberately stood in the pouring rain, thoroughly soaking myself. I invited the students to come and stand in the rain and look at the dark clouds. I got them hooked on the water cycle. The students helped me improvise a funnel-and-test-tube rain gauge to measure the amount of rain. We got so engrossed in the activity that we did not notice the DEO leaving the room. (His evaluation comment on the observation sheet was that I had difficulty in maintaining classroom discipline.)

Dhanasekaran now works as a supervisor at an automobile assembly plant. He is happy with his job, and his daughter recently got married.

What do I remember about you as a teacher? The day you let me take apart your motorcycle engine in the classroom. I offered to do that because my father had a repair shop, and I knew how to do it. Most teachers would have said "No," but you let me take the engine apart. It was the last class period of the day, and the students crowded around watching me. You held each piece from the engine and explained the workings of an internal combustion engine. We had trouble getting your bike started after I put everything back. But none of us had any trouble remembering the parts of an engine.

After I collected 27 of these episodes, I did a systematic content analysis to identify the factors that contributed to memorable learning. I can present you with my list of technical labels, but let me use plain English: All episodes of effective instruction involved trust, spontaneity, accepting offers, listening and awareness, storytelling, and nonverbal communication.

Other days, other times, other topics, and other target groups. The same elements help me teach a variety of technical and soft-skill topics in different corporations around the world today.

These are also the elements explored in Kat Koppett's book.

Kat practices what she preaches. She tells stories about storytelling. She is spontaneous and makes you feel that you can trust her. The subtext of her writing—the nonverbal elements—reassure you that she is listening to your thoughts.

Another word about the structure of the book. There is some debate about which is more effective: Presenting generalizations, rules, and principles, and letting the reader figure out specific applications; or presenting specific instructions and procedures, and letting the reader extract the general principles. Some people prefer to progress from the general to the specific whereas others prefer to move in the opposite direction. Kat lets us have our cake and eat it, too. The first part of the book provides us with six powerful improv principles and their potential applications to management and training. The second part of the book provides tightly structured directions for using 50 specific activities—along with a clear explanation of how the basic principles are incorporated in each activity.

Bravo, Kat! What are you going to do for an encore?

Sivasailam "Thiagi" Thiagarajan
www.thiagi.com

Kat Koppett is a playful, purposeful, powerful pioneer in the burgeoning field of Applied Improvisation. I have had the pleasure of seeing Kat in action in a variety of settings—as part of the Mop & Bucket improv troupe that she cofounded, as part of a TEDx program, and for the past two years as a featured speaker at The HUMOR Project's 54th and 55th international conferences on "The Positive Power of Humor and Creativity." In all these settings, it has been very clear that Kat is very congruent and very competent—she practices what she teaches.

In fact, after she delivered the closing keynote at our conference, I wrote to Kat:

> Our audience from throughout the United States and abroad was totally mesmerized, amazed, and amused with your incredible improv. You had them laughing and learning! The rousing and prolonged standing ovation you generated was a funtastic way to end our weekend. Our audience improvised on the conference evaluations—you and Mop & Bucket received a slew of 10 + 's (and that's on a 1–5 scale)!

You will give this revised edition a standing ovation and a 10 + as Kat shares proven, practical, productive, powerful processes that can invite improvisation in your life and work. This new book piggybacks on the platform Kat built in her groundbreaking first edition.

In the foreword to the first edition, Thiagi said, "Bravo, Kat! What are you going to do for an encore?"

Here is the encore! We need this second edition—now more than ever. In a world beset by accelerating change, we must be able to think on our feet (and on our seat) in our organizations, in our families, and in our own personal lives. The art of improvisation is a vital set of attitudes and life skills for the twenty-first century. Individuals who are not creative and organizations that are not innovative will be left behind.

This book gives you a chance to work and play with the key improv principles of mental flexibility, trust, spontaneity, listening, accepting and building on others' ideas, and performing with presence—all of which will help to inspire your own personal spontaneous combustion creativity and jump-start your organization's ability to innovate. You'll learn how to get out of your own (creative) way and get your creative juices flowing by moving from "Yes, but . . ." to "Yes, and . . ." in life and at work. You will learn terrific, tried-and-true improv theatre techniques to enlighten and light up your life.

This new edition is an E-Z read: it will Enliven, Energize, Entertain, Engage, and Educate you about the power of improv in everyday life and work. Drawing on a decade of cutting-edge work that Kat and her colleagues have done since the first edition, this new volume really expands the range beyond training games to a set of tools to improv (and improve) individual and group performance at all levels and in all contexts.

The first edition mostly focused on training and trainers. Although Kat adds ten new experiential exercises and expands the tips for trainers at the beginning of the second section, this new text goes beyond trainers and recognizes that everyone can be (and needs to be) a performer who calls on improvisational skills and mind-sets to promote productivity and pleasure at work (and in life outside of work).

Kat has also revised and expanded the storytelling chapter to include the latest applied story work of the past decade. In this case, "The I's have it": storytelling is Increasingly touted as an Important, Impactful, Imaginative, Innovative, Interactive, and Insightful educational and business tool. In an age of instant messaging, Facebooking, and tweeting, we need more than ever to recapture the human touch and the magic of storytelling to communicate with charisma. How do you get your message across to your boss, colleagues, customers, students, clients, patients, family, and friends (especially if it requires more than 140 characters)? Chapter 6 will help you to command focus, create compelling stories, hone your storytelling skills, match your message and style to your audience, and see how stories can magically capture attention and increase retention.

I have such great respect and appreciation for Kat. I am honored to have a chance to welcome new readers to the banquet this book offers you . . . and to welcome readers of the first edition back for seconds. There is a lot of new food for thought in this book.

So, let me end this Foreword—and begin this book—with a toast to Kat Koppett and this new edition that supports the notion that learning is FUNdamental—the FUN comes along with da mental.

Jest wishes,
Joel Goodman

Dr. Joel Goodman is founder and director of The HUMOR Project, Inc., in Saratoga Springs, NY. He is the author of eight books, creator of www.HumorProject.com, and recipient of the International Lifetime of Laughter Achievement Award. Joel has done humor and creativity presentations in all 50 states and on all seven continents.

# INTRODUCTION

"We all [improvise] every day—none of us goes through our day to day life with a script to tell us what to do."
—Kim "Howard" Johnson, *Truth in Comedy*, 1994

"My contention is that creativity, now, is as important in education as literacy. And we should treat it with the same status."
—Sir Ken Robinson, TED Talk, 2006

Back in 2001, when Stylus first published *Training to Imagine*, the term *applied improv* was barely in existence, and the idea of using improvisational theater techniques in business settings verged on the wacky. Our publisher showed courage and agreed to publish a book on how to use improv as a training tool, as long as the word *improv* did not appear in the main title. Now, a decade later, there is a global community of practice with annual and regional conferences called the Applied Improv Network. Our collective clients touch virtually every age group and industry. What seemed like a flaky or merely gimmicky approach to organizational development just a few short years ago has grown into a relatively mainstream set of skills and principles embraced by even the most traditional of organizations. At Koppett + Company alone we have designed and delivered programs for bankers, corporate sales forces, physicians, state government workers, engineers, health care workers, academics, and of course trainers and consultants. We have traveled from India to Brazil to Paris to Oklahoma, and anywhere we go we find professionals eager to learn new ways to surf the ever-shifting, twenty-first-century tides.

Why has the professional world, even in its most conservative halls, come to embrace improv? It has become obvious that the world is moving at increasingly fast speeds, with increasingly diverse participation and a set of rules that shift radically and with lightning-fast frequency. Thought-leaders such as Daniel Pink, Rosabeth Moss Kanter, Stephen Denning, Thomas Friedman, and countless others have articulated for us that success in moving forward in our ever-changing world will require a different set of skills from those historically focused on in business settings. As Daniel Pink writes in *A Whole New Mind* (2006),

> The Future belongs to a very different kind of person with a very different kind of mind—creators and empathizers, pattern recognizers, and meaning makers. These people—artists, inventors, designers, storytellers, caregivers, consolers, big picture thinkers—will now reap society's richest rewards and share its greatest joys. (p. 1)

In this context, organizations are looking for ways to develop their creativity, flexibility, and communication skills. And, we have come to believe, improv is uniquely positioned to address those development needs. Why?

Soon after the release of *Training to Imagine*, I got a call from an actor colleague with a lead on some work for a national health-care provider that was looking to bring improv into its patient–physician communication skills program. The company had already had conversations with an out-of-town trainer, but because we were local and connected, we landed a meeting. With all the eagerness and passion of an eager, passionate young practitioner, I pitched the value of improv for the workplace. I am guessing I spewed all of the chapter headings in the book, plus good chunks of text. I quoted studies, I used all sorts of jargon from graduate school, I crafted a brilliant case for how creativity and collaboration skills could enhance outcomes and the bottom line. My potential clients nodded and responded satisfactorily. But then, at last, when I had finished my spiel, there was a pause. "Uh . . ." said one of them gently, "What about the idea that we are all performers, and we are all performing all the time?"

Oh. Yeah. That. The fact that we are, in fact, all improvising all the time—that what we do each day is make up what we are saying and doing, with greater or lesser effectiveness. What a simple and brilliant idea. "Oh, yeah. That, too." I said.

A couple of years later, I met my competitors for that sale, a New York–based group called Performance of a Lifetime. It was they who had provided our client (and by proxy ourselves) with that elegant language. I have since had the privilege of working with their principals on a variety of projects and credit them with furthering my work and the field of Applied Improvisation in general, greatly. What Performance of a Lifetime has taught me is that the case for applying improv to the business (and life) stage is outrageously simple. Human beings are improvisers. We are improvising all the time. Any interaction can be viewed as an improvisational scene in which we are the actors and writers and directors. By studying the principles and techniques of the improviser then, we are just looking to figure out how to do it more effectively. How can we become better at our performances as leaders, team members, teachers, students, parents, innovators, and managers? Duh, improv applies to human interaction at work: Who wakes up to find a script for the day waiting for them on their bedside table?

Improv training in business environments can still be viewed skeptically, of course. Often, when we speak to stakeholders in the design phase, we hear some version of, "Well, I think what you're doing is incredibly valuable and interesting, but you need to understand our people are _____ [doctors, engineers, professors, senior executives, frontline managers, whatever]. They are different." And you know what? The folks who tell us that their colleagues are different are right: Doctors have different challenges and cultures and languages from engineers, who differ from sales people, who differ from teachers. What we all have in common is that we are human beings.

Improv, by definition, does not provide a neat and tidy paint-by-the-numbers script. What it can provide is a set of philosophies and exercises that are remarkably simple and applicable in nearly any situation in which humans wish to effectively build relationships, solve problems, adapt to new circumstances, and create new products and processes.

In that context, *Training to Imagine* strives to present improvisational theater techniques in ways that allow trainers, leaders, and individual contributors of all kinds to adapt to their environments. You need not have a background in theater or a desire to perform to use these tools. All you need is a wish to enhance learning and infuse your environment with creativity, teamwork, and effective communication.

Specifically, this text provides:

- Explanations of the major improvisational theater concepts and techniques.

- Organizational applications of those skills.

- A series of exercises suitable for use in professional development environments.

When I set out to write a revised edition of *Training to Imagine*, I had great dreams of creating a comprehensive and up-to-date text. I realized, though, that those were Sisyphean goals. The field continues to grow so fast that in any given week, I would come across a dozen or more articles and examples that I felt MUST be included here. Ultimately I acknowledged the impossibility of the task and made friends with "better" rather than "perfect." A good improv lesson. That said, I believe this text is improved. In this new edition I have added:

- An expanded section on how to choose the most appropriate activity.

- Additional examples and case studies of applied improv in practice.

- A more explicit focus on leadership and applying improv outside of a formal training setting.

- Updated references.

- Even more activities for leaders, individuals, and groups to employ.

Initially our work and this text focused mostly on the trainer and formal learning environments. Because our work has expanded so much, we hope the revised text will speak more directly to anyone who wishes to develop their own skills or create environments in which their colleagues can do so. Just as you need not be a performer to apply these approaches, you need not be a professional trainer to facilitate these activities. Anyone can bring improv philosophies and techniques to work, through their own individual practices, or by sharing the activities with others. To that end, we have changed some of the language to focus on "leaders" rather than "trainers." We consider anyone who takes action to have positive impact as a leader.

*Training to Imagine* has no illusions of serving as a comprehensive manual for the performing improviser, as a complete list of improvisational game formats, or as a complete guide to effective professional development. It simply aims to offer practical tools and techniques to individuals within organizations who wish to enhance and expand their performance options.

A note on attribution: One of the most daunting tasks I faced in writing this book was tracking the origins of the exercises. The development of improvisational theater has been, itself, improvisational. Someone has an idea or creates a format, and, before you know it, there are companies around the world adapting and building on her inspiration. Intellectual property has become a hot issue with the advent of the Internet, and it remains a sticky one. Improvisers have been struggling with it for years. I have been present for the creation of some wonderful exercises that, only weeks later, I saw attributed elsewhere. I made peace with the impossibility of tracking each activity when Rebecca Stockley, a BATS Improv founder and thought-leader in the West Coast improv community, told me this story.

When she was writing the book *Improvisation Through Theatre-Sports,* coauthor Rebecca Stockley found herself searching for the creators of games, too. Her quest for the origins of one specific game, "Sound Ball," (called "Invisible Balls" on page 179) sent her from person to person for months. She went to the improviser she learned it from. That person sent her to someone else, and so forth. Eventually, she was referred to Roberta Maguire, the woman who brought the Theatresports format from Canada to the western United States. A few days after she received the referral, Rebecca ran into Roberta on a ferry.

"Roberta!" she said, "Just the woman I've been meaning to call. Where did you learn 'Sound Ball'?"

Roberta paused for a moment, thought, and said, "Gee, Rebecca, I think I learned it from you!" Although, Rebecca continued to be as vigilant as possible in her attributions, she realized the Herculean nature of her task. I have attempted the same vigilance, and I recount Rebecca's story not as an excuse for any omissions or mistakes, but as an apology and an explanation. If there is a reader who has better information than I, I would be grateful for any amendments.

What I can be relatively sure of are the general influences on my work. Those influences continue to grow, and so the following list has expanded. My major sources of knowledge and inspiration include:

- Keith Johnstone and the Theatresports® companies around the world. Johnstone's book, *Impro*, is an improv "bible," and the Theatresports communities around the world continue to build on his work.[1]

- Del Close, Mick Napier, Amando Diaz, and the Chicago schools. Del Close was a director at Second City and later the founder of ImprovOlympic. Second City is perhaps the most famous comedy and improv company in the United States, spawning such talents at John Belushi, Bill Murray, Mike Nichols, Elaine May, and scores of others. Close's philosophies have been recorded in *Truth in Comedy*.[2] As a student at Chicago City Limits in New York, I became one of many who have inherited the work of Close, Paul Sills, and others, who developed the improv lexicon in Chicago. The next generations of teachers from the Chicago tradition continue to move the art form further in exciting ways.

- Viola Spolin, whose book *Improvisation for the Theatre* may have started the modern-day improv movement.[3]

- My Applied Improv colleagues and friends—too many to mention, but you should look them up at www.appliedimprov .net. In the consulting and training world, improvisers cross-pollinate and share as much as they do as performers. Since the initial publication of this work, my understanding of it has grown tremendously due to the feedback, extrapolations, additions, and revisions of my brilliant and generous professional partners.

- The members of Unexpected Company, Freestyle Repertory Theatre, BATS Improv, and The Mop & Bucket Company, with whom I have explored and continue to explore the craft of improv.

The power of improv as a development tool resides in its experiential nature—its ability to connect people to their intuition, their bodies, their whole brains, and each other. My hope is that the practices in *Training to Imagine* will be engaged in, not just read about. With that in mind, let's get started.

# SECTION ONE

# Principles

# 1

# THE PRINCIPLES

"The techniques of the theater are the techniques of communicating."[4]

—Viola Spolin, *Improvisation for the Theater*, 1983

"Hey, could you read this letter on stage?" the young man says. He
proffers a note written on lined binder paper. "I want to propose to my
girlfriend tonight. I thought you could read this to her on stage, and
ask her to marry me."

"Sure! Anything, man," responds Kenn, an improvisational actor
scheduled to emcee the evening's show. He is experienced and confident. The code says to make the audience happy. Plus, the assignment
sounds great. Romantic. Exciting. Good theater.

A half hour later Kenn is on his knees in front of the proposee. With
the urging of her boyfriend, she has volunteered to come up on stage,
where she has played a scene with Kenn. They are now at the top of an
imaginary hill, resting their legs after an imaginary bike ride. She is
being proposed to by proxy. Kenn reads the letter. "Kelly," it says, "you
are the most beautiful woman I've ever met. I love the way you care for
people and are so generous and kind. I would like to share the rest of
my life with you. Will you marry me?"

There is a pause. "Well?" Kenn says.

"Uh . . ." For a moment the woman is unsure. Is this real? She looks
out at the audience.

"I need an answer," Kenn says, the tickle of panic beginning at his
scalp.

"Uh . . . no," Kelly responds.

At this point, most of us would probably have cut our losses, and, embarrassed for ourselves and the less-than-blissful couple, ushered the woman to her seat. Not so with Kenn. He was committed. He was going to accept whatever the woman said and continue on with the scene. As if it were himself he was fighting for, he persisted.

"No?! Why not?" he says.

"I just don't feel that way about you," she says to Kenn, caught up herself in the role-play.

"Is there someone else?" he asks. The improvisers cringe backstage and look around for a vaudeville hook.

"Yes," she says. The woman says "yes" in front of an audience of strangers!

"Who?" Kenn asks.

"This guy at the gym," she says.

"What's his name?" Kenn astonishingly pursues.

"Hank," she replies.

Improvisational actors—improvisers—make up scenes, songs, stories, entire plays, on the spot, with no script or planned scenarios. They work collaboratively in front of paying customers who expect to be entertained and amazed, with only their skills, philosophies, and colleagues to guide them. Sometimes the results seem magical. Sometimes they feel disastrous. Only through the willingness to risk failure, though, are improvisers able to delight audiences with their successes. The secret improvisers know is that the "failures"—as in the previous scene—can be as satisfying and useful as the successes.

Does the job of an improviser sound familiar? Not so different from everyday life, right? Rather like surviving in the contemporary business culture. Increasingly, the world of corporate America is looking like the world of improvisational theater. The script is constantly being reinvented. The opportunities to plan deeply before acting are becoming fewer, shorter, and less reliable. Not coincidentally, in recent years businesses have begun to realize the value of consciously fostering creativity and teamwork within their organizations. The techniques, philosophies, and exercise of improvisation, then, are a rich source of learning for them.

Often people ask how improvisers can "rehearse" if they don't know what is going to happen in a show. Like athletes, improvisers practice skills that can be used in a variety of situations. They work on expanding and strengthening their abilities, even though they do not know what the specific events will be in an individual game. The fundamental skills that improvisers develop are:

- Trust

- Spontaneity

- Accepting Offers

- Listening and Awareness

- Storytelling

- Performing With Presence

Let's take a look at what these entail and how they might apply to the workplace.

## Trust

The heart of collaboration is trust. Without it no oratory will be convincing, no agreement solid, no relationship productive. This truth is evident to the improviser, as it is to police partners or army buddies. When you willingly walk into danger with nothing but your colleagues to protect you, you had better trust those colleagues. Perhaps it is a little extreme to compare performers to military personnel at war. I certainly would not want to diminish the bravery and importance of those men and women. But improv certainly *feels* dangerous. So, improvisers demand that they have colleagues that they can trust, and they have developed exercises (and tests) to build it.

Team members in any field can use these activities. Sometimes the workplace can feel like a war zone, too. Competition is rampant; casualties are reported every day; daring acts of bravery are required. It is no longer enough to be on the "leading edge." Now we aim to live on the "bleeding edge." Imagine then, how important it is for leaders, managers, and trainers to create an environment of trust when they are virtually sending their people into battle.

# Spontaneity

From a very early age, most of us are taught to censor ourselves. Good thing, really: Without the ability to control our impulses, make judgments, and choose when and if to act, we would be crippled. We could not learn to read, eat with utensils, or shed our diapers. Civilization, itself, is a set of agreed-upon limits we place on our uncensored actions. However, there is a price. We spend so much time exercising our judgment muscles that our creativity muscles can atrophy.

In order to create, a person needs to trust his impulses and follow through on seemingly irrational, nonlinear, or "foolish" ideas. Although the abilities to evaluate and critique are important, if they are out of balance with our abilities to brainstorm and take risks, creativity is sadly impeded.

In improv, there is no time to evaluate. By definition, improvisation is creating in the moment without the ability to revise. Improvisers practice getting out of their own way, so that they can recognize and use their innovative ideas. What is especially interesting about unleashing one's impulses is that it is often the ideas that seem the most dangerous or the most obvious—the ones that our rational mind would have us censor—that yield the greatest fruit. If Kenn, in the scene recounted previously, had followed socially acceptable restraint and refrained from questioning his audience volunteer, everyone might have been more comfortable, but the resulting scene would have been much less compelling and memorable.

# Accepting Offers

When we practice being spontaneous, we learn to accept our own ideas. It is equally important to accept others' ideas. Teamwork of any sort depends on both our ability and our willingness to do that. In improv, ideas and actions—words, physical actions, character attributions, musical accompaniments, lines of dialogue—are called "offers." Anything your partner does or says is an offer. In a moment, an improviser can accept or reject myriad offers. Improvisers learn early that if you do not accept whatever is offered to you, you can spend loads of time searching around for something better, and never get anywhere. All you have got when you are improvising are the current offers. There are no other plans or guideposts. Nothing else exists.

The correlated truth in business is more applicable than one might expect. Often, organizations lose speed and opportunities because ideas are rejected (or merely nominally accepted) when there is value to be had. Saying "yes" sounds good, but can be hard in practice. People reject ideas without fully exploring them all the time, for many reasons. New ideas may mean more work, people fear that someone else will get more credit, the idea feels risky, someone thinks he has a "better" idea of his own. However, every time we say "no" to an idea instead of "yes," an opportunity is lost. That does not mean, of course, that evaluation is not useful. Or that we should commit to every idea. When we depend on our judgment muscles exclusively, though, we throw the baby out with the bathwater, the electricity out with the lightbulb.

There is another step to accepting offers in the improv world. Just saying yes, as powerful as it is, is not enough. Improvisers live and die by the "Yes, AND . . ." rule. "Yes, and . . ." means that not only must I, the improviser, accept an offer, I must build on it. I must contribute. I must make an offer of my own in response to my partner's. It is this process that harnesses the power of collaboration. Everyone offers and accepts. Each team member is responsible for both contributing to and supporting the group's activity. Through the implementation of this method, brainstorming sessions lead to innovative solutions. Even the smallest spark can be fanned into illuminating flames.

## Listening and Awareness

It is impossible to accept and build on others' ideas if we cannot recognize them. By enhancing listening and observation skills, teams and individuals can harvest significantly more ideas, increase their understanding of each other, and communicate more effectively.

Improvisers have the pressure of having to listen and react in front of an audience. They worry not only about what they must say next, but how they will look, how people will judge them, and not falling off the stage. These concerns diminish the ability to sense and build on offers. The feelings improvisers can have on stage—self-consciousness, pressure to get things right, not wanting to make a fool of themselves— are different only in intensity, not in kind, from the pressures that many of us feel most of the time. So many internal and external realities vie for our attention. Keith Johnstone, the founder of Theatresports, and a beloved and admired improv teacher, dedicates much of his work to combating the fear that can blind performers to offers that are terribly obvious to passive observers.

Most people are both more and less aware than they think they are. We take in an extraordinary amount of information that we ignore, and at the same time, our inability to really pay attention can confound our sincerest attempts to communicate. The good news is that listening and general awareness are muscles. They can be developed and exercised.

## Storytelling

Why is narrative so important? All communication, it can be argued, is storytelling. The way humans make sense of facts is by creating narratives that link bits of data to each other and to past experiences. Audiences, then, are constantly looking for stories to help them understand the information being presented to them, and to keep them interested. As long as an audience is wondering, "What happens next?" they will continue to watch.

Audiences may leave a performance remembering a funny line, but the improviser who uttered it will tell you that it was the team's ability to create a compelling narrative that sustained the show. Lots of the climactic moments that audiences remember are only satisfying because of the context surrounding them, many of the characters only defined and adored because of the situation in which they behaved. Charna Halpern and Del Close, the great Chicago improv guru, say, "The most direct path to disaster in improvisation is to make jokes"[5] (Halpern, Close, & Johnson, 1994, p. 26).

Like cotton candy, an improv show with gags and no stories can be delicious for a bit, but quickly becomes unfulfilling. Among other things, if you are going to present an entire evening of jokes—as many stand-ups do—they had better be really, really good jokes. That is why comedians can spend years perfecting a single line. Improv, of course, does not provide that opportunity. In an attempt to offer their audiences (and themselves) turkey dinners in lieu of cotton candy, many of the most respected improv companies have turned to new show formats that allow them to create performances with longer, more complex story lines. And even within the most traditional "short-form" structures, storytelling opportunities are increasingly more sought after.

Storytelling, both within the world of applied improv, and completely independently, has become a widely recognized leadership competency. Thought leaders such as Stephen Denning have been championing it as an invaluable tool for increasing influencing skills, knowledge-sharing, building organizational culture, and learning of any kind. By incorporating stories into communications, leaders can increase their ability to inspire and clarify action. By incorporating storytelling activities, a trainer can support the unconscious process of story creation, thereby enhancing the participants' attention and ability to retain information. Storytelling can be used for everything from increasing presentation skills to building teams to reviewing technical processes to motivating employees. And the best news is that we humans are hardwired to think narratively, so getting better at soliciting and telling stories is a goal we can ALL achieve.

## Performing With Presence

As we know from presidential debates, there is much more to being a good communicator than the words we use. A sneer, a peek at a watch, sweat, all can have more impact than the content of the arguments. That is why so many corporate executives have begun to hire media trainers. A tilt of the head, an "um" or an "ah," or a smile can define our trustworthiness and our character.

Although we may feel sheepish about judging books by their covers, we most certainly do. In a famous treatise on trustworthiness in communication, *Silent Messages*, Albert Mehrabian found that when people perceive a contradiction between the words, the tone, and the physicality of the speaker, they believe the words least of all and measure nearly all of their faith in the speaker's trustworthiness by the tone and physical appearance (vocal cadence, gestures, clothes, facial expressions) of the speaker.[6]

Perhaps these observations are not as superficial as the phrase "judging a book by its cover" might suggest. Just as our subconscious is evident in our dreams, it reveals itself in our bodies. There are lots of exercises improvisers use to increase their ability to be heard, to be relaxed in front of people, to support their content with their tone of voice and physical expression. Without these abilities, no matter how good they are at making verbal offers, performers will be unable to convey a variety of characters or convince an audience of their authenticity.

An interesting subset of the behaviors that improvisers explore and play with (nonverbally and verbally) falls under the heading of "Status." Johnstone, in his seminal work, *Impro,*[7] devotes a substantial section to the topic. Exercises designed to recognize and manipulate status behaviors have become some of the most enlightening and useful techniques to translate into business settings.

In general, if we think of ourselves as performers and track how we are presenting ourselves in any given moment, we expand our range of options and our abilities to achieve our goals.

As such a rich source of creativity, communication, and collaboration techniques, it is not surprising that companies tap improvisation as a source for organizational development. The following chapters will explore these principles and offer ideas, exercises, tips, and techniques designed to expand your improvisational mind-set and exercise your improvisational "muscles."

Just say, "Yes."

# 2

"Sky diving without a parachute is suicide. Total freedom is suicide. . . . Holing up in a closet is vegetating. Total security is vegetating."[8]
—Gordon MacKenzie, *Orbiting the Giant Hairball*, 1996

## The Principle

There is a statistic, perhaps apocryphal, that has floated around for years, that says that people are more afraid of public speaking than they are of death. A workshop participant insightfully pointed out that the reason for that may be that a public speaking engagement seems, for most of us, more imminent. When it comes down to it, we might rather get up in front of people and talk than meet our maker. But research does point to the fact that getting up in front of others and expressing oneself can cause extreme amounts of stress. When you are presenting with a team, then, you had better trust the folks on stage with you.

Diane Rachel, a coach and performer with BATS Improv in San Francisco, offers an improv course entitled "Sex and Violence." It is designed to get students comfortable doing scenes that include the most taboo and dangerous subject matter. Why? Because that taboo and dangerous subject matter is the stuff of great theater. We go to the theater, since the time of the Ancient Greeks, for catharsis—to experience the terror and sadness and exaltation and adventure that most of us avoid in real life. So what is it that Rachel is teaching when she teaches a course titled "Sex and Violence"? Ultimately, Rachel's class is mostly about building trust among a group of performers. Trust grows through

- acknowledging discomfort,
- establishing and enforcing ground rules, and
- engaging in an activity together.

The last item, actually participating, makes the real difference. Ultimately, the only way to engender trust is to show, through your actions, that you are trustworthy. The only way to do that is to act.

This does not mean that you must wait until the moment of crisis—a fire, a war, a performance, a sales call—to build trust. There are plenty of small cues that people read in order to assess whether their teammates and managers should be trusted. Every action, every word, whether directed at us or at those around us, gives us a clue to the trustworthiness of our colleagues. Much of improv rehearsal time focuses on creating trust—helping individuals become more focused and empathic and providing the group members opportunities to build rapport.

John Phillips of Synectics suggested the following formula to define *trust*:

$$\text{Trust } f \frac{(\text{Credibility})(\text{Intimacy})}{\text{Risk}}$$

In this model, *credibility* is defined as perceived competence—seen as possessing the knowledge, skills, and abilities necessary for the task. *Intimacy*, in this context, translates to empathy, the capability to understand, identify with, and care for others. When people believe that someone possesses these two qualities, their trust for him will increase. The last piece of the formula states that the higher the perceived level of risk, the more credibility and intimacy are needed to engender trust.

In business, a lot of formal attention can be focused on assessing credibility. How well does this person perform? How much do they know? Trainer credibility is gained through subject-matter knowledge and group-process skills. If a trainer has no experience in a given industry, that community might question her more. Similarly, if her slides are crowded or confusing, her capability might be doubted. A leader's or manager's credibility might come from holding a certain degree or having experience within a given industry or having attained success on certain projects. In all cases, credibility feels easy to measure and to increase through training and experience.

Intimacy, at first glance, seems harder to identify and develop. Isn't empathy just a personality trait that some people possess or something that grows naturally with time?

Improvisers believe that empathy is a skill. And they have devised exercises to cultivate it. And that is great news for organizations as evidence, from the work of Daniel Goleman and others, mounts that emotional intelligence is at least as important a predictor of success as IQ.

In *To Kill a Mockingbird*, Harper Lee's (1960) classic novel of life in a small Southern town, Atticus Finch says to his six-year-old daughter, "You just learn a single trick, Scout, you'll get along better with all kinds of folks. . . . You never really understand a person till you consider things from his point of view. . . . Till you climb inside of his skin and walk around in it." That is a pretty good definition of *empathy*. It could also define the acting process. Actors learn how to identify with characters and get inside their skins, so to speak. The farther they are from the character, the better. Many actors love to play villains, because the "bad guys" are often the more complex and intriguing characters. Interestingly, actors will often say that they do not see their villain personas as evil at all. Once they have understood the character's pain and motivations, no matter how vile we may think they are, the actors speak of them with affection.

In real life, too, the better we know each other, the greater the chance we will empathize. Traditionally, organizations have aggressively divided what they deemed the "professional" lives of their employees from their "personal" lives. But increasingly, businesses are recognizing that this dichotomy is not only false, but unhelpful. In fact, the more team members know about each other, their colleagues, and their constituents, the more effective they can be. And as companies and work groups become more diverse, the attention one must pay to getting to know and understand one's colleagues increases. It used to be that the "Golden Rule"—treat others as you like to be treated—

proved a dependable way of guessing and meeting others' needs. Now, organizational development practitioners speak of the "Platinum Rule," which says, "Treat others the way *they* wish to be treated." The distinction inherent in this modern-day framing is not superficial. It acknowledges that although as humans we might desire the same things at a fundamental level, in practice, how we measure and experience those things (e.g., physical well-being, respect, community, purpose) might show up in radically different ways. For example, in her TED (technology, entertainment, and design) talk on "The Art of Choosing," Sheena Iyengar (2010) shares a story about attempting to order sugar with her green tea while living in Japan. The waiter and eventually the manager refuse to serve it to her, because putting sugar in green tea is just not done! When Iyengar defends her desire, the staff goes so far as to tell her that the restaurant does not have any, rather than accede to her request. However, when Iyengar gives up the argument and orders coffee instead, it arrives with two packets of sugar on the side of the cup. As Iyengar puts it,

> The American way, to quote Burger King, is to "Have It Your Way," because, as Starbucks says, "Happiness Is in Your Choices." But from the Japanese perspective, it is their duty to protect those who don't know any better . . . from making the wrong choices. (Iyengar, 2010)

So, true empathic interaction may not be as easy as we initially think. On the other hand, the effort to empathize can, in and of itself, have impact. Building trust begins with expressing a desire to build mutually respectful relationships, and simply investing in asking about others can reap great rewards on both sides. As Corey Jamison, of the Kaleel Jamison Group, a consulting company specializing in creating cultures of inclusion, says, "Inclusion begins with 'Hello.'"

A first step to building trust involves consciously providing opportunities for colleagues to learn about each other. Try this: At a meeting or training, ask participants to exchange the stories behind their names—first name, last name, nickname, whatever. For example, Kat is short for Katherine. I got the name Katherine because my mother had always been told she looked strikingly like Katharine

Hepburn. My father made up the name Koppett, and there are still only four of us in the world. He was born in Russia, and when he became a sportswriter in the 1950s, he changed his surname to Koppett because our original family name, Kopeliovitch, was constantly mispronounced, and, he said, it wouldn't fit on the newspaper's byline. (Sadly for him, Koppett is also constantly mispronounced. It's KOP-it, like "Stop it.")

This straightforward exercise spurs conversation and reveals professionally appropriate but personal details that individuals often have not thought to share. Participants report that it is a low-risk exercise, and in the United States especially, names unlock such varied histories. As innocuous as they may seem, these small bits of information begin to weave a net of safety and connection that allows empathy to grow and trust to develop. "Your dad was a sportswriter? How 'bout them Mets?" "I LOVE Katharine Hepburn. Don't we remind you of the women in *Desk Set* sometimes?" "I always wondered how you pronounced your last name."

Another getting-to-know-each-other activity, "Stats," is a variation on musical chairs. Participants sit in a circle, with one chairless person standing in the center. The person in the middle shares a fact about himself. Anyone to whom that fact also applies must get up and find a new chair. Those are the only rules. We have found that this simple game produces great delight. There are a couple of wonderful things about it. First, it creates an environment in which the participants themselves control what they reveal about themselves and decide what they wish to learn about others. Second, the exercise is designed so that it is not the most aggressive or most vocal people who are in control. In fact, it might turn out that the more retiring team members find themselves in the center of the circle more. This enables those who might not otherwise have a voice to lead the discussion.

Getting to know each other makes it more likely that we will not only pay attention to each other, but that we will support each other. "Make your partner look good" is an improv mantra. It means, concentrate on your partner rather than on yourself and take responsibility for both of you. "If your partner drops the ball," we say, "it is *your* responsibility, not his." What a difference when team members interact this way. "Ball Toss" physicalizes this concept. Participants stand in a circle and toss a ball in a repeated pattern so that each person receives and throws the ball once. Once the pattern is established, the facilitator adds more and more balls, increasing the level of difficulty. Finally, the participants are instructed to walk around randomly while maintaining the same pattern. At first, groups struggle. Team members throw balls without looking to see if their partner is ready. People blame each other for dropping balls. Sometimes, participants try to confuse each other by throwing especially fast or high. However, when the facilitator tells them that the *thrower* is responsible if the ball does not get caught, things change. People focus on their partners rather than on themselves. They make eye contact before tossing the balls. They aim and throw gently. They call each other's names to get their partner's attention. *Accountability* became a corporate buzzword early in this century. Ironically, the conversation often devolved into one of admonitions directed at others, as in "YOU should be more accountable." By focusing on making your partner look good, leaders, managers, and individual contributors can separate true accountability from thinly disguised blame.

Earlier in the chapter we talked about how Diane Rachel built trust in her "Sex and Violence" workshop by acknowledging discomfort, establishing and enforcing ground rules, and having her students practice together. Using improv games, it is possible to see trust improve before your eyes. The use of an "icebreaker" admits that there is ice to be broken—it acknowledges discomfort. Games of all sorts provide a structure or set of rules within which people can play with security—they set ground rules. And the more you play, the more comfortable people become—games work as practice for higher-risk situations.

It cannot be said too often: Whether in the context of daily interpersonal activity or in a workshop setting, trust is the foundation upon which everything rests. If you wish for workshop participants or team members to make themselves vulnerable, you must nurture their efforts regardless of the outcome. The following chapters present a variety of concepts, all of which are capable of enhancing creativity, positive communication, and collaboration. None of them will amount to anything unless the environment is imbued with trust.

# The Principle in Action

As trainers, managers, and leaders, we require people to follow our advice and procedures. In order to be effective, we must be deemed trustworthy. In addition to incorporating trust-building activities into our work, the following are some ideas for enhancing trust.

## Practice What You Preach

The "Do-what-I-say-not-what-I-do" school of guidance has been shown to be ineffective. If you have enough authority, people might comply, but they will not trust you. If you encourage people to take risks and then punish them when they fail, they are even more unlikely to risk than if you had never brought up the topic.

A teambuilding consultant I know used to ask his employees to deliver parts of his training workshops as part of their professional development. "This is your bit," he would say. "I trust you. Design it however you wish." Then, when the moment came, he would interrupt and contradict them in front of the workshop participants. Needless to say, trust eroded very quickly. And the effect was only exacerbated when he spoke of trust the next time.

## Recognize That You Are Seen

Human beings are highly attuned to potential danger, and they judge situations by what has happened to others before them. It is the monkey who saw the previous monkey eat the poisoned berry, and therefore avoided eating it himself, that survived. Every interaction that you have affects not only the person whom it involves, but also everyone who sees the event or hears the story.

In the previous example, when the consultant undermined his trainer, he sabotaged not only her trust in him but the trust of his other employees. They heard the story and became nervous about training with him. Plus, the workshop participants doubted the consultant. They saw what he was doing. If he was not going to support his own people, why should they believe him when he said they should take care of each other? And why should they feel safe participating in his activities or asking questions? It is frighteningly easy to build a reputation. Build the one you want.

## Set Expectations

If direct reports or students are unclear about what it is you want of them, they can feel undermined, even when that is not your intention. The more straightforward you can be about the procedures and outcomes you expect, the more likely it is that people will succeed. You will not have to go back on your word. They will not feel confused or wrongly attacked if things veer off track. It is wonderful to offer people freedom to create and problem-solve in their own way. However, if there are specific results you are looking for, you had better explain them from the beginning. Perhaps if the consultant had set more specific expectations of his trainers, for example, he would not have felt the need to jump in during the workshop.

## Frame Your Intentions

We are aware of our intentions, whereas others can only guess at them based on our behaviors. By "framing," or setting context for your actions, you can defuse mistrust born of misinterpretation. Studies of attribution theory show that people will forgive harmful actions if they believe the intentions were honorable. For example, if I arrive late to a meeting, other attendees may assume that I do not think their time is valuable. Or they may assume I am unreliable. If I let them know that I was in a car accident or, less dramatically, if I apologize for keeping everyone waiting and let them know that I respect them and their schedules, I can mitigate the damage. That does not mean that actions will be excused time and time again, but in individual instances, sharing your intentions can avert the erosion of trust. Let people know why you are requesting something. Tell them why you made a particular decision. Articulate the need, as you see it, for whatever process you have employed.

## Provide Low-Risk Opportunities

If you ask people to take huge risks without establishing yourself as dependable, you are likely to be rebuffed. Find small ways to reassure people before you embark on high-risk activities. As mentioned, games are great tools for accomplishing this task. Another technique is to have one-on-one conversations with those you are coaching—conversations devoted only to uncovering their needs and concerns. On the simplest level, let people know you are willing to listen, before you ask them to. Yet another strategy is to give people easy tasks that they feel comfortable with before challenging them, so that they can trust their own competence, and you can trust your ability to be supportive.

## Pick Your Activities Carefully

Some of the most powerful training activities are jolts. A *jolt* is an experience designed to dramatically challenge a participant's attitudes or beliefs. Jolts can create useful epiphanies. They can also leave participants feeling vulnerable, manipulated, or betrayed. In choosing to use these kinds of activities, weigh the payoff against the price. Like a physician, a trainer's responsibility is first to do no harm. Sometimes, a trainer chooses a certain activity, not because it is the best way to facilitate learning, but because she enjoys the ease or status that accompanies running it. Be clear about why you are employing an activity that requires manipulation. Is it necessary to consciously mislead the group or set them up to fail? Can you get the same value from a less confrontational experience? Remember, trust is even harder to rebuild than to build.

# ☞ Key Points ☜

- Trust is the foundation for all creative and collaborative endeavors.

To establish trust:

- Acknowledge discomfort.
- Establish and follow ground rules.
- Practice together.

$$\text{Trust } f \frac{(\text{Credibility})(\text{Intimacy})}{\text{Risk}}$$

- Make your partner look good.
- Practice what you preach.
- Recognize that you are seen.
- Set expectations.
- Frame your intentions.
- Provide low-risk opportunities.
- Pick your activities carefully.

# 3

# SPONTANEITY

"Spontaneity is the moment of personal freedom when we are faced with a reality and see it, explore it, and act accordingly."[9]
—Viola Spolin, *Improvisation for the Theater*, 1983

"As soon as you say 'failure is not an option,' you've just said, 'innovation is not an option.'"
—Seth Godin, "The Flip Side," 2011

## The Principle

One of the staples of improv training is a game called "Soundball" (see "Invisible Balls," page 179). The exercise is taught in many beginning improv classes, played as a warm-up in virtually all improv companies, and used in applied improv workshops around the world. In "Soundball," the participants stand in a circle and throw an imaginary ball back and forth. Each time a participant tosses the ball, she makes a sound. Her partner, the person to whom she has thrown the ball, repeats the sound as he catches it. There are no rules about what kind of sound to make, no parameters around what sounds are acceptable or prohibited. Anything goes.

At first, learners often express a surprising amount of discomfort playing "Soundball." After all, there is no real ball, so one need not be coordinated. The exercise demands no specific sounds, so one cannot fail. But regardless of the lack of skill required or of rules of right and wrong, people find all sorts of ways to evaluate their input.

"How many people worried about creating a 'good' sound?" the facilitator asks. At least half the participants raise their hand.

"How many thought that one or more of the sounds they made were 'bad'?" Almost as many cop to this.

"Who felt that someone else made a better sound than they did?" Everyone laughs and nods.

"What were some of the reasons you judged your sounds as bad?" the facilitator probes.

The participants pipe up, "It was too soft." "It had too many consonants." "It was too similar to the sound I made the first time." "It wasn't *interesting*."

"Soundball" highlights the arbitrary nature of our judgments. Usually, when we reject a product or an idea, we feel we have substantial reasons for doing so. We would love to say "yes" and follow our impulses, but they are wrong! The idea is just bad! "Soundball" illustrates how capricious our internal judge can be.

Learning to identify and follow impulses is the foundation of creativity. Virtually all literature on initiating the creative process counsels this: Find ways to stimulate yourself and then spew forth ideas without evaluation. There will always be time to edit later. Julia Cameron, in her classic, *The Artist's Way* (1992), recommends that those who wish to be more creative write three pages of uncensored, unshared prose each morning. Anne Lamott, in her spunky and supportive book on writing, *Bird by Bird*, encourages "shitty first drafts"[10] (pp. 21–22). Business consultants and creativity experts all talk about separating idea generation from evaluation, about engaging in divergent processes before converging on a solution. That spontaneity is an important ingredient for creative output is well known. Embracing spontaneity in practice, however, can be a struggle.

We are trained from the earliest of ages to resist our impulses, and of course, this can be a good thing. We don't want our children (or ourselves) to wear diapers forever. Patience and self-discipline and aligning ourselves with social convention (a.k.a. emotional intelligence) set the foundation for success in life at least as much as IQ does, and they are skills that must be learned and practiced (Goleman, 1996). But it is all too easy to throw that diaper-wearing little bundle of spontaneous babyhood out with the bathwater.

Most of us have some story about a parent or a teacher somehow discouraging our creative impulses. Johnstone, writing in the late 1970s, railed against educational institutions for destroying innate creativity.[11] As our cultural norms have changed, we might be shocked to hear that a teacher told our children that they cannot color their trees orange, or instructed them to mouth the words to a song rather than to sing along with the group. However, we often cut arts programs completely and trumpet curricula guided by standardized tests—a move away from autonomous learning and creative thought. Even as we recognize creativity and flexibility as important foundational skills for the twenty-first century, we force educators to restrict, criticize, and control learning environments. Sir Ken Robinson is one of the most vocal advocates for reforming our whole educational system. He makes no bones about the fact that he feels traditional education misses the mark: "Imagination is the source of every form of human achievement. And it's the one thing that I believe we are systematically jeopardizing in the way we educate our children and ourselves" (Robinson, 2006).

In business settings, the same sorts of contradictions persist. Movements to support creativity have been growing in business settings, and yet there are many companies that resist. Why? Edward Deci and Richard Flaste, authors of *Why We Do What We Do* (1996) and experts in self-determination theory, assert that in order to be intrinsically motivated, a person must have confidence, autonomy, and a sense of belonging. As explained by Matthew Richter of The Thiagi Group, Deci and Flaste advise that teamwork, empowerment, and opportunities for self-expression result in higher worker satisfaction and therefore in higher productivity and retention.[12] Ironically, though we know intellectually that spontaneity is desirable, actually being spontaneous can feel like a threat to all three of the important aspects of motivation just mentioned. If we do not know how and why we are responding in certain ways, how can we feel confident of our competence? If we do not evaluate our ideas before we articulate them, how can we have a sense of control—even over ourselves? If we are willing to think and act outside of the generally agreed-upon parameters of a situation, what guarantee do we have that we will be accepted?

Although many of us profess to dislike repression, when it comes down to it, we are not sure we want more freedom. Johnstone claims,

"Most people I meet are secretly convinced that they're a little crazier than the average person"[13] (p. 83). If that is what we believe, do we really want to let others in on the fact? If we, ourselves, were really free to do and speak and think, unfettered, then what would we learn about ourselves? What would we be compelled to follow through on? How would we know if we belonged?

In addition, some of us like the idea that creating is hard work—that only the most brilliant, tenacious, and experienced individual can come up with the next best product or process. If spontaneously following our most ludicrous or most mundane whim is the way to success, then what kind of security does seniority and expertise offer?

An improv colleague of mine shared the following story, illustrating the threatening aspect of spontaneous creation. We had just performed the opening night of a new, completely improvised musical format, "Spontaneous Broadway." Her father, a classically trained musician, expressed both amazement and doubt about our show. "You couldn't really have improvised all that," he claimed. "You must have planned the story. At least you already knew the music, right?" My friend had been improvising for years. Her father had heard about her endeavors for close to a decade. He had seen plenty of shows. But when he saw a group of improvisers succeed at creating songs with structure and rhyming lyrics and metaphors and melodies, he was dumbfounded. Composing was supposed to be difficult. If this ragtag group could do it on the spot, what did that say about him and his colleagues? How could he value his years of education and toil?

In other words, being spontaneous is both the most natural and the most difficult of behaviors. It is both delightful and risky. So, for trainers and leaders in business settings, there are two questions: Do we wish to foster spontaneity (read: creativity and adaptability), and if so, what can we do to support it?

I assume for now that the answer to the first question is "yes"—at least in theory, at least in some contexts. The case for the increasing importance of creativity in the workplace due to accelerated timeframes, increased competition, and new markets and technologies has been documented repeatedly, and you must have picked up this book for some reason. Let us discuss the second question: How can individuals and organizations become more spontaneous?

The following are the improvisers' secrets for creating environments that foster spontaneity.

## Spend Time Exercising the Spontaneity Muscle

Use warm-up exercises to get the juices flowing, before applying your creativity where it counts. Through games and exercises that are "content-less," individuals can practice following their impulses while the stakes are low.

## Provide Structure

Create a structure within which individuals can feel free to explore. As Gordon MacKenzie points out in the epigraph for chapter 2, there are limits to the amount of freedom that is useful.[14] Sometimes too few restrictions, even if the result is not actually dangerous, can inhibit creativity. Laura Livingston says that her job as the artistic director of Freestyle is to provide the jungle gym for the performers to swing on. To this end, many of the formats improvisers have developed set parameters within which the improvisers must create. By limiting the options, and focusing on creative attention, improvisers can feel grounded and inspired, rather than unmoored. The limits themselves provoke ideas. In professional contexts, the same applies. Be clear about your objectives and parameters. Not only do explicit restrictions not have to hamper creativity, often they can inspire it (think Apollo 13).

## Do Not Censor

Just because we say we are in idea-generation mode, we do not automatically shut down our inner judge. The internalized voice of our parents, our teachers, our managers, and our peers can be very strong. Terry Sommer, my first improv teacher, once said, "If you can't think of anything, it's because you're censoring what you're thinking of." Sometimes, our internal judgments are so powerful that we stifle our impulses even before we are aware of them. We censor ourselves because we think we will be deemed inappropriate, stupid, silly, or dull.

If not by others, then by ourselves. In *Zen Mind, Beginner's Mind*, a book on Zen meditation and practice, Shunryu Suzuki suggests that the beginner is closer to the ultimate Zen state than practitioners who have been meditating for years, because they have no preconceptions about the right way to meditate or what their experience should be. He says, "In the beginner's mind there are many possibilities, but in the expert's there are few"[15] (p. 21).

The following are some specific tips for bypassing your censor:

- Be foolish. Risk sounding silly. That's the whole point, really. For an idea to be creative, it must be somehow fresh, either in content or application. But, ideas that are new, by definition, challenge the status quo. It is those ideas that are most likely to be dismissed. How many stories are there of genius ideas being rejected? Van Gogh sold one painting his entire lifetime; the Swiss scoffed at the crazy idea of digital watches; even Einstein scorned quantum theory.

  As much as we say we value creativity, often what we mean is that we value the successful results of creative endeavors. People who create have a special gift. Not talent, I would offer—some do, some don't—but courage. If we are going to "think outside the box," then, like a Jack-in-the-box, we must pop out of one, not hunch protected inside.

  Finally, let us look at the word *foolish* itself. The fool in the archetypical sense is the innocent, childlike in his curiosity. And his power lies in his willingness to take risks. The universe protects him as he takes "fool-ish" risks, indulges in sensual plea- sures, and discovers new, exciting adventures. It was the fool in the royal courts who not only entertained the monarchs, but also was able, through wit and charm, to tell truths that the most powerful advisors feared relaying. A willingness to be silly is the key to the fool's power, and to our creative selves.

- Be obvious. Nothing will kill the creative process quicker than trying to be "creative," and trying to be "interesting" is a surpris- ingly ineffective way to come up with original thoughts. When you search for something "original" you reject idea after idea that pops into your head because it is obvious TO YOU. "Well that's dull," you think. Or "Everyone else must have already thought of this." Or "That was too easy; it must be stupid." The truth is, what is obvious to you is the most organic, authentic impulse. That means it might also be the most valuable, because it is probably based on what is happening in the moment. By trusting the obvious and articulating it, there are two possibilities: You are voicing something that everyone is thinking, but no one else has the courage to say (for example, the child who tells the emperor that he has no clothes); or something that seems very obvious to you, but no one else has thought of.

An example of the latter remains legend at Freestyle Repertory Theatre. During a Theatresports performance, Laura Livingston and her team were challenged to do a scene in which someone plays an inanimate object. Laura accepted the challenge and asked the audience for a location in which the scene could take place. Someone shouted out, "a zoo." Let's pause here. Take a moment to list all of the inanimate objects that come to mind. Got them? There are lots, right? Laura thought of something immediately. It was the only thing that came to mind. In fact, she was a little worried that if she didn't speak first, someone would take on the role of the only obvious choice, and she would be left with nothing. She rushed to take her place and start the scene. What object did she choose to be? Monkey poop. That's right, a monkey's excrement. Needless to say, no one else had thought of that particular object. But Laura swears it was absolutely the first and only thought in her head. The scene, by the way—between the monkey and his poop—was very funny and rather sweet. And it was much more "original" than whatever Laura might have come up with by rejecting her first idea as either too obvious or too gross.

## Celebrate Failure

In *The Art of Play*, a drama therapy text, Adam and Allee Blatner say, "Permitting yourself to plunge into improvisation can be helpful by reminding yourself that in play there is endless room to make 'mistakes'. . . . Allow what might otherwise seem like a mistake to become transformed into an opportunity for further creativity"[16] (n.p.). The only way to maximize creative risk is to celebrate the brave failure as well as the triumphant success. If failure is punished, then the risk of risking is just too high. Of course, there are times when following an innovative path will result in defeat. That defeat must be acknowledged and valued as a necessary cost of implementing the right process, or the process will be discarded with the result.

A favorite story that I have heard from a number of creativity consultants recounts how a vice president at IBM during its heyday was summoned to CEO Tom Watson's office after an innovative project of his had failed miserably and cost the company more than $10 million. The VP's colleagues had warned him off the project from the beginning, but he had fought for it, rejecting the current wisdom and taking a wild risk. Now, all the naysayers had been proven right. The mortified employee handed Watson his resignation upon entering the office. "What's this?" Watson asked.

"My resignation," the VP replied.

"Your resignation!" Watson said. "You can't resign. We just invested $10 million in your education" (Leman, 1996, p. 202). Now that's supporting failure.

The best part of embracing failure is that failure is not just a necessary evil. It can result in the most exciting ideas of all. Books on "mistakes" that became huge successes, like *Mistakes That Worked* (1991) by Charlotte Jones and John O'Brien, have proliferated in the last decade. Perhaps you have heard that Post-it notes were the result of a failed attempt to make a traditional adhesive. Alexander Graham Bell set out to create a hearing aid. Flubber was intended to be a new energy source. Improvisers talk about "mistakes as gifts." Sometimes failures can offer the greatest rewards.

## The Principle in Action

There are substantial payoffs for increasing spontaneity in the workplace, not just in a formal brainstorming session, but in any moment when you wish to capture something new, fresh, or honest. The concept of not censoring input during the divergent portion of idea-generation and problem-solving sessions has become commonplace. However, as we have discussed, even during formal sessions set aside for brainstorming, offering up ideas without judgment is easier said than done. Trainers and leaders can support the process in a number of ways. And, what many trainers and leaders have already implemented in formal idea generation sessions can prove just as important to other aspects of professional life.

At this writing, the idea of recognizing failure as a necessary ingredient in building an organization that can learn, grow, adapt, and create has taken hold. Thought leaders, such as Kathryn Schulz, Seth Godin, Rosabeth Moss Kanter, and Ken Robinson in the Harvard Business Review, TED Talks, and Fast Company have touted a willingness to fail as a necessary quality of innovative organizations within the last year alone.

## Create a Developmental Environment

As trainers and instructional designers, we often have conversations about creating a safe environment for learners. What we realized at some point was that "safe" should not mean "comfortable." An environment that supports growth is one in which individuals feel all right being uncomfortable. It is only when discomfort is acceptable that people can stretch and develop. Creating such a space for being comfortable with discomfort involves the following:

### WARM UP

Before asking people to generate content or learn new skills, engage them in warm-up activities. Through games like "Invisible Balls" (page 179) or "Word Drill" (page 233), participants can practice circumventing their censors in risk-free situations. Just like athletes stretch physical muscles before running, participants can warm up their creativity and problem-solving muscles before focusing on a specific issue.

### SEPARATE IDEA GENERATION FROM IDEA EVALUATION

If you want to encourage spontaneity, especially in an atmosphere that generally has rules, processes, and tangible measures of success (like the bottom line), you must create the space for ideas to be born and nurtured without testing and examining them too closely at first. Having officially sanctioned brainstorming sessions is one way to accomplish this. Another is to hang out with colleagues after hours at bars. You would be amazed how many show formats were created in these venues.

The opposite is also true. Evaluation is not a bad thing. If individuals feel that they will be stuck with crazy ideas, they will not share them. Assuring participants in idea-generation sessions that there will be time to examine and assess at another time will allow them to offer and accept wild ideas in the moment.

## REMIND PEOPLE OF THE RULES OF THE GAME

When asking for ideas, reiterate the rules of the divergent phase of creative problem solving:

- Table evaluation

- Quantity over quality

- Record ideas without discussion

- Build on previous ideas

Be vigilant about insisting that group members stick to these rules. As soon as someone begins to evaluate an idea, the safe space for generating risky ideas can be poisoned. If a group feels uncomfortable, they might try to censor individuals who are not censoring themselves.

A note here about formal brainstorming: As anything else, idea-generation sessions can be done well or badly, and because they are sometimes done haphazardly, without enough focus, preparation or follow-up, the process of formal brainstorming has attracted some criticism of late. Additionally, as the study of creativity and innovation has grown, evidence has emerged that much real innovation and creative problem solving happens outside of the formal idea-generation session. We do not take this to mean that brainstorming sessions are not valuable. Although solutions may emerge in other settings at other times (the importance of incubation, or down time, is increasingly recognized, for example), gathering people together to focus on a problem, hear each other's ideas, and seed new ways of thinking adds to the soup out of which innovation emerges. Regardless, recognizing your impulses, daring to notice and express your "irrational" thoughts, and separating the generation of ideas from the evaluation of ideas can be thought of as "muscles" that benefit from a workout in any context.

## PROVIDE ESCAPE HATCHES

It is possible to devise ways for participants to abdicate responsibility for their ideas. This allows people to separate themselves from something that sounds foolish or risky and, therefore, makes them more willing to share those ideas. The simplest method for detaching individuals from their ideas is to make the input anonymous. Have people write down ideas and post them. Have them write ideas on 3"x5" cards and exchange them. Invite small groups to brainstorm and then share their ideas collectively.

Another technique is to provide virtual "masks" or alternate personas. For example, while brainstorming ideas for making meetings more effective, I have asked clients to think about what Oprah might do, were she running a meeting. Or Arnold Schwarzenegger. Or Mickey Mouse. Or the CEO of the company. Or their wackiest relative. In that context, participants can share ridiculous thoughts and say, "Hey, *I* don't think that is a good idea, but Mickey Mouse might." Other sorts of "what-if" scenarios can be used to similar effect. "What if it were the year 2020?" "What if money were no object?" "What if people had no hands?"

## REWARD HONESTY

As leaders, managers, and trainers, we must allow people to voice confusion and resistance to our ideas; otherwise, we will not be able to gauge the real effect of our communication. Often, those contrary thoughts are the kinds of thoughts that individuals may censor when faced with a power differential. When I taught English to Russian immigrants, my students would nod and assure me that they understood the lessons, even when they had no idea what I was talking about. They had been taught that the way to get by in school was to pretend to understand, publicly do whatever the authority figure said, and then cheat. This tactic may have worked in terms of avoiding conflict or circumventing bureaucracy, but it certainly did not help them learn. I found that I could help the students by saying, "I will not continue until someone asks me a question." Eventually, my students and I invented "Stupid Simon." Students would say, "Kat, *I* do not have a question, but Stupid Simon would like to know . . ." (Stupid Simon became a virtual mask).

Spontaneity games also work to gather needs. Many of the games we have discussed—"Stats," "Invisible Balls"—can be modified to contain content. For instance, in training sessions play "Invisible Balls" tossing "The reasons you are here" or "Skills you expect to gain." In informal settings ask, "What do you wonder about that you think you should already understand?" "If I forced you to come up with an objection to this plan, what would it be?"


## Recognize That When You Are Sure You Are Right, You Are Wrong

In the exploding field of neuroscience, as well as in current sociological and psychological arenas, a profound truth has emerged: We are terrible judges of reality. Our experiences of the world are stunningly limited and skewed. In *Mistakes Were Made (But Not by Me)*, for example, Carol Tavris and Elliot Aronson explore research on cognitive dissonance and the deep impact it has on our lives individually and collectively. They say, "Most people, when directly confronted with proof that they are wrong, do not change their point of view or course of action but justify it even more tenaciously" (2007, p. 2). Christopher Chabris and Daniel Simon, in their entertaining and accessible book *The Invisible Gorilla* (2010), discuss half a dozen "cognitive illusions," including the Illusions of Attention, Memory, Confidence, Knowledge, and Potential, that interfere with our assessment of ourselves and situations we find ourselves in. So, what do we do with this knowledge of our limitations? Many of these processes cannot be overcome by simply knowing they exist. But, ironically, knowing that we are fallible can help us. We can seek out other opinions, supporting research and technology. We can be open to new ideas.

*Wait, what? Is this whole chapter touting the value of spontaneity? And now we are saying that our impulses and insights are wrong?* Why should we trust our spontaneous impulses when we are so flawed in our cognition?

Two reasons:

1. If we remember that those little judging voices in our heads are biased at best, and most likely misguided, we allow ideas and insights to be aired and explored before they are internally evaluated and killed. We are as likely to reject useful stuff as to promote dreck.
2. When we evaluate ideas, we must get better at doing so rigorously. By separating the process of generating ideas and sharing instincts and impulses from the process of analyzing, choosing, and assessing impact, we can get more value out of both processes. The censoring, judging, and assessing that arises impulsively should not be trusted. Save that process for a time and place when personal opinions can be verified and tested. In the meantime, let the impulses flow. Who knows what gems are in there?

As much as we have focused on the stress of spontaneity, spontaneous expression can feel exhilarating. Implementation of these tools and techniques will contribute not only effectiveness, but joy to your work.

## Behind the Scenes

Being willing to be spontaneous is not an easy task, no matter how many years you spend working on it. The most experienced improvisers I know will admit that what has changed over the years is not that the little judging voices in their heads have gone away, but that the performers have become more willing to ignore them. Even as I am writing about spontaneity, I am aware how insistently the editor in my head judges what I write. It will not be assuaged by promises of later revisions or reminders that no one will have to see this draft. It plagues me. Here are just a few of the ways I am tempted to censor myself:

"You can't write that. It's too . . .
. . . risqué
. . . obvious
. . . artsy
. . . business-y
. . . literary
. . . clichéd"
"You can't include that. Your colleagues will
. . . disagree
. . . feel competitive
. . . be embarrassed
. . . think you are self-aggrandizing"
"Your mother will
. . . criticize your grammar
. . . misunderstand
. . . think it's bunk"

What do the judges in your head say?

## ☞ Key Points ☜

- Spontaneity is at the heart of creativity.

- Spontaneity is risky.

- Socialization kills spontaneity.

- To increase spontaneity:

  - Do not censor.

  - Be foolish.

  - Be obvious.

  - Celebrate failure.

  - Separate idea generation from evaluation.

  - Recognize the arbitrary nature of judgment.

  - Build the jungle gym.

  - Warm people up.

  - Reiterate the rules of brainstorming.

  - Provide escape hatches.

  - Reward honesty.

  - Recognize you are wrong.

# 4

# ACCEPTING OFFERS

"What would happen if we *agreed* instead of disagreed? Problems would be solved and there would be more action"[17]
—Charna Halpern et al., *Truth in Comedy*, 1994

"The big question is whether you are going to be able to say a hearty yes to your adventure."
—Joseph Campbell, *The Hero With a Thousand Faces* (n.p.)

John Lennon met Yoko Ono at a showing of her artwork in New York. He browsed and eventually came upon a magnifying glass that was hanging from the ceiling. Below it, Ono had placed a painter's ladder, and Lennon climbed the ladder, took up the glass, and held it to a tiny message written on the ceiling. The single word scribed there was *Yes*. Lennon said that it was that piece, with that specific word, that kindled his interest in Ono.

The most important, fundamental rule of improv is: "Say, 'Yes, and . . .'." It is the principle by which improvisers live, and arguably every other principle is simply a subset of this master tenet. "Yes, and" means accept what is offered by your partner (or the environment) and build with it. "Yes, and" is a phrase that is ubiquitous in the improv community. Johnstone discusses the power of "yes, and-ing." "Yes, & Productions" is the ImprovOlympic producing organization, and www.yesand.com is a major discussion forum for improvisers around the world. I believe the phrase, as well as the concept, originated with Viola Spolin in her book *Improvisation for the Theater*.[18]

"Yes, and" is both an incredibly simple and a deeply profound tool for solving problems, building relationships, and creating new products. Organizations have embraced the concept more directly and enthusiastically than any other improv approach, and applied improv practitioners continue to expand its usefulness in developmental situations. Let's break it down and take a look.

Through my collaboration with the folks in the applied improv community, and most specifically with the principles of Performance of a Lifetime, I have come to understand the "yes, and" rule in two distinct ways.

The first is the more literal, and it is the way it has been initially understood and implemented by organizations: Be more positive, say *yes* more, look for the places to agree. Spontaneity, which we discussed in such great detail in the last chapter, can be seen as internal yes, and-ing. It can be defined as a willingness to accept what our minds and bodies are offering us. Accepting and building with *other* people's ideas is the next step. For some of us that proves much harder. For some of us, perhaps it is more comfortable. But ultimately, what improvisers know is that if we are going to work collaboratively, at some point we must "yes, and" to ourselves and our partners, because that is all we've got.

Take a look at this illustrative activity, based on Johnstone. "But Versus And" is played in two rounds. In round 1, five volunteers are asked to plan a company picnic or holiday party. After the first suggestion is made (for example, "Let's have the party in Hawaii."), each successive idea must begin with the words "*Yes, but . . .*". It usually goes something like this:

"Let's have the party in Hawaii."

"Yes, but . . . that's so far away."

"Yes, but . . . we could take a plane."

"Yes, but . . . some people don't like to fly."

"Yes, but . . . they could take a boat."

"Yes, but . . . that would take too long."

"Yes, but . . . we could have the party ON a boat, like a cruise!"

"Yes, but . . . some people get seasick."

"Yes, but . . . you're all wimps!"

Entertaining, perhaps, but not much of a party plan. If the exercise does not conclude in an argument, it tends to degenerate into lots of discouraged and silent participants staring at each other and the facilitator, devoid of ideas. Everyone is relieved to sit down.

In round 2, the volunteers try again. They are invited to complete the same task—planning a company party—with one variation. This time, instead of starting their sentences with "Yes, but . . ." they begin each offer with the words, "*yes, AND* . . .". With the adjustment, the dialogue progresses in this fashion:

"Let's have the party in Hawaii."

"Yes, and . . . let's have a big roast pig."

"Yes, and . . . those little tropical drinks with umbrellas."

"Yes, and . . . leis."

"Yes, and . . . we can charter a jet to take everyone there."

"Yes, and . . . we can have fruit and poi for the vegetarians."

"Yes, and . . . alcohol!"

"Yes!" (Everyone seems to be for alcohol.)

"Yes, and . . . we'll get Sam to dance in a grass skirt."

"Yes!"

This time, the participants report feeling happy, enthusiastic, and relaxed. (Even Sam.) Observers agree that this sounds like a much more enjoyable party to attend. Everyone understands that saying, "yes, but . . ." is just a cagey way of saying, "no." Gerald Neirenberg and Henry Calero, the authors of *How to Read a Person Like a Book*, say, "'But' is a verbal eraser" (1971, p. 57). Nothing that comes before it counts. Whereas saying, "yes, and . . ." allows the team members to accept and build on others' offers.

In improv, any idea is better than no idea. Because the entire show is being made up on the spot, all an improviser has is what he and his fellow improvisers agree on in the moment. There is no reality, except for the mutually accepted one. As long as someone rejects what his partner offers, a scene will stall, and a new idea must be found to jump-start it. Paul Zuckerman, a producer at Chicago City Limits, used to say that refusing to say "yes" is like incessantly driving down the highway and never taking an exit. A scene (or a project) cannot get started until you commit to a destination. Sure, there may be other towns down the way, but you will never discover the treasures in any of them, unless you choose one to visit.

Accepting offers is just as important in non-improv settings. Ultimately, saying "yes" is the foundation of all relationships. What is flirting, but a way of saying, "Yes, I see you, and I like what I see"? Negotiation is finding the solution that meets all parties' needs—that each side is willing to accept. The sales process consists of getting the customer to say "yes" to whatever it is you are selling.

There are subtler rewards for saying "yes," too. Team members become sullen, demotivated, and uninspired very quickly when their ideas are consistently rejected, whereas when their ideas are accepted motivation increases. Individuals begin to feel more competent and a stronger sense of belonging when those around them accept their ideas. Even in the three minutes of participating in the "But Versus And" exercise, in which the stakes are nonexistent, participants begin to feel frustrated or invigorated, depending on the pattern. Improvisers have labeled the rejection of offers "blocking," and it is the ultimate taboo in their world. In the world of business, blocking does not hold the same stigma, but the results—resentful and dissatisfied colleagues—may be the same.

Most people will buy into the concept that saying "yes" is valuable in theory. We like our ideas to be accepted, at least to the extent that they receive consideration. But in practice, most of us are quick to say "no." Why?

- Saying "yes" requires action.

- Someone else might get more credit than we.

- Someone we don't like is championing an idea.

- Contradicting or debating is a way we have learned to feel smart.

- The idea offered feels risky/silly/unoriginal (see chapter 2).

- There is a perceived or actual lack of resources.

- We think the idea is "bad."

- We think the idea is impossible to put into practice.

- We like our own idea better.

- We don't understand the idea.

- We don't recognize that an offer has been made.

- Conflict is exciting.

In *Impro,* Keith Johnstone says, "There are people who prefer to say 'Yes,' and there are people who prefer to say 'No.' Those who say 'Yes' are rewarded by the adventures they have. Those who say 'No' are rewarded by the safety they attain"[19] (p. 92). Often it may be that simple. Saying "no" feels safer. Less to do. Less to think about. Less to risk.

Don't get me wrong. There are GOOD reasons to say "no." Sometimes the reasons just listed are legitimate. If my daughter asks to go play with her friends in the middle of the freeway, I will say "no." There are pitfalls to knee-jerk agreement (i.e., group-think) as well. But for many of us, our "no" muscles are significantly more exercised than our "yes" ones. So, we err on the side of blocking others' ideas and experiences, rather than looking for opportunities to build.

In other words, sometimes we say "no" out of habit. We are simply more experienced at it. In the 1990s, business schools started teaching creativity courses. Michael Ray, a Stanford Business School professor, offers a course called "Creativity in Business." As one of the first to design such a course, he speaks about why he felt teaching creativity was so important. His students could easily come up with 15 reasons why an idea would not work, and that, he says, bespeaks a great deal of intelligence and creativity. Rarely, though, did it enter the students' heads to apply the same talent to generating ideas or devising solutions to potential challenges in the ideas presented (Ray, 2008). All their training and socialization has been geared toward finding the problems, seeking out the weak links. If we actively look for value—offers to like, offers to agree with—we are more able to build, solve, and create. Sue Walden, of ImprovWorks, cues her clients to employ this positive mind-set by responding to another's ideas by starting with the phrase, "What I like about your idea is . . ." If you are looking for it, there is almost certainly something of value to find.

Let's pause here for a moment and investigate this word *offer* that has been bandied about.

*Offer* is an improv term for anything that exists or is created by your fellow improviser. An offer can be verbal, physical, conceptual, or emotional. If an actor walks into a scene, fumbles with the door, and says, "Hi, honey, I'm home," the offers inherent in the moment include:

- the words—the fact that she has labeled this place as *home*, and another actor as *honey*.

- the specific tone of voice—is she happy, sad, tired, frustrated, triumphant, casual?

- the objects she may be carrying—does she have bags, an animal, papers, a knife? (N.B.: often improvisers create "space objects" rather than using real props, because they can't know ahead of time what they will need. Fellow improvisers must be aware of the objects created along with everything else.)

- her fumbling with the door.

- the way she walks.

- the way she holds her head.

The number of offers is almost infinite. Any of them can be accepted, ignored, or rejected.

Which brings us to the second, and perhaps even more interesting interpretation of "yes, and." You see, although improvisers do talk about being positive, and finding agreement, "yes, and" does not mean that I have to literally "agree" with every idea or offer. Many entertaining scenes have characters in them who fight or have different points of view. At bottom, what "yes, and" means to the improviser is "see, hear, receive" as much information as possible and accept and build with that—because, just because, it exists. Whether we like it, agree with it, expected it, the offers that have been made are all we've got. As Performance of a Lifetime puts it, "It is the improviser's obligation to ask, '*How* can I accept and use this offer?' not '*Will* I accept it?'" (Performance of a Lifetime training course). In real life, looking at "yes, and" as a process of recognizing, accepting, and building with what exists—not what we wish existed—results in powerful creative and strategic juice.

In this context, not acknowledging or using an offer is called "blocking." We block for all of the reasons listed previously and, perhaps most often, because we fail to see the offers in front of us (see chapter 2).

Encouragingly, improvisers have discovered that "Ye ███ even when others block. The best improvisers (and most ███ lem solvers) are virtually impossible to block successfully. Alain Rostain, of Creative Advantage, suggests in his idea-generation sessions that participants think about a block, or objection to an idea, as a springboard for new ideas, rather than as a wall. Once this adjustment is made, a block becomes simply another offer.

My favorite example of an improviser accepting a blatant block and diffusing it happened in a scene about a divorced couple fighting over custody of the children. Early in the scene, Gerri Lawlor, one of BATS Improv's biggest crowd-pleasers, had pulled a gun on the actor playing her ex-husband and suggested that he hand over their child. The gun was, as was referenced previously, imaginary.

When Gerri first put up her fingers, as if holding a gun, the husband lifted his hands, backed up, and said "Take it easy!" The offer of a gun had been made and accepted. Later in the scene, however—perhaps because he thought it would be funny, perhaps because he couldn't think of anything else to say—the actor turned to Gerri and said, "What is that in your hand, anyway? That's not a gun." Big block. Everyone, onstage and off, held their breath.

Without missing a beat, Gerri replied, "It *is* a gun. I put a milk carton over it so that it wouldn't scare the kids."

Gerri accepted the offer inherent in the block (that the gun was unrecognizable) and maintained the reality of the scene. She continued to honor all of the events and assumptions that had come before. She was able to accept her partner's offer by justifying why he might not have thought the gun was a gun. Plus, she justified it in a way that enhanced the scene, by focusing on the mother's relationship with her child, the heart of the scene to begin with. The improvisers present that night analyzed and praised her skill. The audience just cheered with glee.

Successful collaboration requires Gerri's sort of ebullient optimism. People will say "no." Those individuals and teams who believe they can overcome the obstacles will try harder, give up less easily, and consequently achieve more. In his book *Learned Optimism*,[20] Martin Seligman discusses the value of an optimistic outlook. Although studies show that pessimistic individuals might view the world in a more "realistic" way, optimists tend to succeed more often, simply because they expect to. He states that ". . . organizations, large and small, need optimism; they need people with talent and drive, who are also optimistic. An organization filled with optimistic individuals—or studded with optimistic individuals in crucial niches—has an edge" (p. 255). Specifically, Seligman suggests that individuals in the following fields need optimistic approaches: "sales, brokering, presenting and acting, fundraising, creative jobs, highly competitive jobs, high burnout jobs" (pp. 255–256). That covers an awful lot of people. The good news, according to Seligman—as you may have divined from the title of his book—is that optimism can be learned.[21] Improvisers believe so, too. Since the first publication of this text, an entire field of Positive Psychology has emerged from the work of Seligman and his colleagues, and the value of focusing on strengths rather than attacking weaknesses continues to gain support.

Once we decide to accept offers, the muscle is easy to exercise. In "Yes, and . . . Story," players tell a story by adding one sentence each, beginning the sentences with the words *yes, and.* . . . The activity has the dual advantage of helping participants practice both recognizing and creating with others' offers. In a story, as in real life, one must tease out the offers, keep track of the larger context, and only then choose how to contribute.

Another of my students' favorite "yes-anding" activities, "Accept This!" (a.k.a. "It's Tuesday," page 127), is described in Johnstone's book *Impro*. In it, one person makes a neutral or "boring" offer, and his partner over-accepts that offer.[22] Over-accepting consists of responding as if the offer were incredibly important and then building on it to an outrageous degree. When the second person reaches a conclusion, the first person over-accepts some boring detail of that person's rant and continues. It might look something like this:

Person A: "Here's your coffee."

Person B: "My coffee! Oh, my coffee. What a glorious elixir! My life's blood. Ah, I cannot live without coffee. I was just about to quit, because I had no energy to go on. But now I can continue. The project will be complete, the company will not go bankrupt. I love coffee! I love YOU! You brought me my coffee, and I love you. Can you stay for a while? Have a seat."

Person A: (Over-accepting the neutral offer) "Have a seat? Have a seat?! I . . . I don't know what to say. No one has ever asked me to sit down before. I spend all day running around, bringing people coffee. Wow. You want me to sit down? Here? In this chair? This beautifully cushioned, leather chair? Oh, I couldn't. I just . . . (he begins to weep with joy.)"

And so on.

"Accept This!" is a terrific exercise for pointing out the power of emotion. It underlines the fact that accepting offers is as much about having an enthusiastic attitude as it is about the specific response. It is also great practice in saying "yes" first and figuring out why later.

Another simple "yes-anding" activity is "Expert Interviews" (page 164). The familiar format and slightly less hysterical genre make it a preferred choice when working with traditional or slightly reticent clients. A talk-show format is set up with a host and a guest. The guest is assigned an area of expertise, and the host interviews him. The expert is instructed to feign extreme confidence and answer every question in the affirmative. The interviewer is instructed to respond as if she is very impressed and to "yes, and" the expert's statements by allowing her questions to be inspired by the last answer. The directive to say "yes" to all questions produces wild results, and students may resist at first. When coached consistently, though, they submit, and the results are delightful.

"So, you've written a book," the interviewer says.

"Yes," the expert responds.

"I see it's called, *Dating Tips for the Shy Giraffe.*" (The group has given the guest the topic of "animal husbandry," and the performers have begun to talk about "animal husbands." From there, they get to animal dating.)

"Yes, it is. *Dating Tips for the Shy Giraffe.*"

"What's tip number one?"

"Bring flowers." (The expert answers quickly, even though he later says he wanted to censor his answer as too obvious.)

"Flowers, ah, yes, wonderful. And why is it so important for shy giraffes especially to bring flowers?"

"Well, if there's something there to eat, you don't have to talk."

The students laugh appreciatively. The expert swears that he did not have any idea where he was going to end up. But by simply saying "yes" to his interviewer's questions—and to his own impulses—he created a satisfying and entertaining interchange that was successful in ways he could not have anticipated ahead of time.

So, what about real life? Let us take a look at a couple of examples in which saying "no" seems to be the only option. Can we use the power of "yes, and" in constructive ways?

Previously we used the example of my daughter asking to play in traffic. Obviously I am not going to agree to her suggestion. This is a clear "*no*-is-the-right-answer" situation, yes? But if we look a little deeper, are there offers we can accept? She says she wants to go with her friends to play in the middle of the freeway. First, what offers are there? Perhaps she:

- wants to find a new, fresh activity.

- wants to go on some wild adventure.

- wants to impress her friends.

- likes cars and wants to be near them.

- is fascinated by traffic patterns.

- wants Mommy's attention, because she sits at the computer writing for hours.

Any of those desires provide "yes, anding" opportunities. I will not "agree" to let her play in traffic, but I could design a scavenger hunt in the house. Or take her to a car show. Or show her an aerial view of traffic in Bangalore. Or put the computer away and cuddle.

William Ury, coauthor of the paradigm-changing *Getting to Yes* (Fisher, Ury, & Patton, 1991), the book that introduced the concept of win–win negotiating to the general population, more recently wrote a book called *The Power of a Positive No* (2007). He wrote it, he said, because he looked around at all the efforts to get to "yes" in a win–win manner and thought, "Yikes! What have I done?!" He saw example after example of people undermining their own best interests, or acting against their own values in service of what they thought win–win meant. In *The Power of a Positive No*, then, Ury puts forth a Positive "No" if you will. He says, "In contrast to an ordinary No which begins with No and ends with No, a Positive No begins with Yes and ends with Yes" (p. 16). The first "yes" refers to our fundamental values or commitments, or "interests," in Ury's language. In the previous example, it is my daughter's safety and well-being. Any position that threatens that core value, I should not say "yes" to (i.e., playing in traffic). So the second layer of the yes sandwich is a "no." "No, I will not let you play in traffic." I should be willing to assert my power in defense of my first "yes."

It is the third layer that provides opportunity. It says, now that I have protected my baseline value, what CAN I find to say "yes" to? This is the layer of "yes, and." I might not agree with you, but I will make the effort to assume value in your offers and look for ways to build with them. Ury calls the third "yes" an Invitation and suggests it builds relationships.

Imagine the following scenarios:

- Your boss asks you to stay late AGAIN.

- A direct report rolls her eyes when you ask her to do something.

- Your colleague suggests an idea for a project. You tried a similar thing two years ago, and it was a disaster.

- Your sales force is promising timeframes that manufacturing cannot meet.

- Your mother-in-law wants to move in.

What are the offers being made? What are your own interests and values (i.e., the offers you are making to yourself)? Given that, where can you assume value in the offers your partner is making, rather than simply blocking? What can you build with?

## Drawing It Out

*"Yes, anding . . ." is not only a verbal process. "Paired Drawing" is based on a Johnstone exercise, "Eyes."[23] Participants are asked to draw two dots, which serve as eyes, on a shared piece of paper. Then, in pairs, they draw a face, alternating back and forth, contributing a line or feature, each turn. As soon as one of the sketchers hesitates, the drawing is finished. Then two artists, alternating one letter at a time, title it. Charles Schwab employees created the following examples as part of a team-building session in San Francisco.*

# The Principle in Action

The more power an individual has, the more it matters whether she rejects or accepts ideas. A manager who kills the suggestions of his direct reports will soon find he has a staff devoid of ideas or initiative. A trainer who ignores the input of her students will fail to impart her material. Here are some methods for applying the "Yes, and" philosophy.

## Assess and Strengthen Your Personal "Yes, and" Ability

If you wish to encourage certain behaviors, there is no better place to start than with yourself. Start to track your own reactions. How often do you accept others' ideas? When do you say "no"? Check your analysis with those who report to you. Do they perceive you to be as open as you expected? If you find yourself blocking offers more than you want to, try to figure out why. Take a look at the list of reasons people say "no" listed previously and see which ones strike a chord. You might also want to assess the environment in which you work. Do you feel like your ideas are accepted? If not, how do you react?

Take the time outside the workplace to practice your "yes, anding" skills. Make up "yes, and" stories. Imagine saying "yes" to ideas that you have previously rejected. Pause and reflect on your reasons before saying "no" to ideas. See if there are ways to use your resistance as a springboard to a solution that builds on the idea. Pledge to explore at least one stupid idea a week.

## Look for Value

Andrew Kimball of Qube Learning, a Silicon Valley consulting firm specializing in human performance, tells this story. Consolidated Foods was looking for ideas for new candy products. In one of their brainstorming sessions, someone came up with the idea of "candy that could talk." The idea was recorded, but rejected by most people as ridiculous and impractical. It wasn't like you could get tape recorders that small, even if people would be willing to swallow them. An executive in the group, however, was taken with the concept and pursued it. Upon further investigation, he found out that his chemists had been working on a process for encasing carbon dioxide in a sugar shell. When placed in water these small pellets would explode, making crackling and popping sounds. In other words, they talked. The CEO devoted lots of resources to the project, and "Pop Rocks," which had one of the most successful new candy debuts in history, was born.

It is not enough to generate original ideas. Those ideas must be nurtured and brought to fruition. Remember, it is not the ideas that seem practical and safe that need a champion. A "yes, and" mind-set is most important when you don't initially agree or see obvious value. When you do, "yes, and" is automatic.

## Enhance Teamwork

Teams that accept and build on each other's ideas are more creative, more collaborative, and have less unproductive conflict. The "yes, and-ing" exercises in this book will enable teams to practice supporting each other, maximize their creative output, and build trust. Simply being aware of when team members are accepting and when they are blocking can help a group work more effectively together. Often we are blind to how much we reject without exploration. By bringing a conscious focus to this aspect of their interactions, team members can work to build trust, risk taking, problem solving, and a sense of common purpose.

## Motivate

As mentioned in chapter 3, self-determination theory suggests that the elements of intrinsic motivation are perceived needs for competence, autonomy, and relatedness[24] (Richter, 2001). Accepting and building with individuals' offers enhance motivation in all three areas. Learners will feel more competent if a trainer acknowledges and builds on the skills they already possess. When employees have their ideas valued, they feel both a sense of control over their environment and a sense of affiliation with those who accept them. In general, team members who feel their experience and input is valued will be more engaged and happier.

☞ **Key Points** ☜

- Accept offers and add to them by saying, "yes, and . . .".

- Spontaneity is a way of saying "yes" to yourself.

- "But" is a verbal eraser.

- An "offer" can be anything.

- Saying "yes" is the bedrock of all relationships.

- We can come up with all sorts of reasons to say "no."

- Saying "no" (blocking) is a well-developed habit.

- Blocking can be overcome.

- Optimism is the willingness to overcome obstacles and continue to say "yes."

- Remember your "yes" sandwich.

- Assess and strengthen your own ability.

- Look for value.

- Enhance teamwork.

- Motivate through acceptance.

# 5

# LISTENING AND AWARENESS

"Imagining should be as effortless as perceiving."
—Keith Johnstone, *Impro*, 1979

Close your eyes. (All right, open them, or you won't be able to read.) Imagine the keypad on your cell phone. What words, numbers, symbols, and colors are displayed there? Are there letters along with the numbers as there are on a traditional keypad? What letters correspond to the number 4? What happens when you make a call? What appears on the screen?

Before an offer can be accepted, it must be recognized. Not as easy a task as one might think. There is so much information bombarding us in any given moment that to make sense of it, we blot out and distort the data. We make choices about what to focus on. Who has time to study her cell phone screen? Why bother? And yet, what important information do we miss—by not listening to instructions, not hearing feedback, not recognizing discrepancies between what we believe and what exists?

As we discussed in chapter 3, our perceptions of the world are deeply flawed. We will never be completely accurate trackers of data or "reality." We look for what we expect. (For some revelatory fun on this topic, see Christopher Chabris and Daniel Simons's Invisible Gorilla experiment [2010].) We look for things to confirm our assumptions and self-concept. (Check out *Mistakes Were Made [But Not by Me]* by Carol Tavris and Elliot Aronson, 2007.) Often, we simply do not (or cannot) perceive much of what is going on around us.

Dr. Francis Crick, one of the two scientists who mapped the structure of DNA, went on to study the brain. He has been quoted as saying, "80% of what we experience as true we make up." Even if the statement is only 20% true, it leaves us plenty of room to doubt ourselves.

Remember playing "Telephone" as a kid? You would whisper a phrase into someone's ear, and they would whisper it to someone else, and so on, until it came out in some mangled version at the other end. Many of us played that game for entertainment, but did we internalize the lesson? Amazingly, in everyday life, we expect to be able to understand and pass on messages without distortion.

That said, we can be more aware of how much we miss. Organizations have taught courses on listening skills for years and suggest relatively simple techniques for increasing retention and understanding. They include asking questions, checking understanding by feeding back information, and taking notes. Most of these techniques come down to an acknowledgement that our memory, retention, and understanding are untrustworthy at best. We advocate using support strategies like these whenever possible.

Not every situation lends itself to the use of such methods, though. And not every offer can be captured in this way. As improvisers, we rarely get the chance to double-check our assumptions or write down details before moving forward. To successfully create coherent stories and songs instantly, we must track and retain all sorts of details—objectives, attitudes, past events, names—in the moment, the first time around. So, improvisers approach listening and awareness as muscles that can be exercised and strengthened. We work on our ability to focus and to see, hear, and retain information, just as a basketball team would work on passing and making free-throw shots.

"Story Exchange" (page 214) serves both as a workout for listening muscles and as a jolt, highlighting the complexity of listening well. Participants pair off and take turns telling a short story from their lives. Then, they switch partners and each person tells the story that they just heard, as if it were their own, trying to repeat the words, gestures, and inflections of the story as accurately as possible. Again, the participants switch partners, telling the story that they heard most recently. Finally, the entire group comes together, and each participant recounts the last story told to him or her. At the end of this process, not one of the stories is completely accurate. Some are so different as to be unrecognizable.

"Story Exchange" illustrates the frailty of our listening, understanding, and retention skills. But improvisers who practice listening notably improve their ability to recount the stories accurately. Chris Oyen, one of my first improv coaches at Chicago City Limits in New York, amazed me one night when I was babysitting his two-month-old daughter. Rebecca was a beautiful but colicky baby, and she was screaming. The Mets were playing a game on TV. The dog was snoring, and Chris was passionately discussing an event that had happened at the theater the night before. After about a half hour of this mayhem, Chris's friend came in from the kitchen and asked me, "What's the score?" I had no idea. It had been at least twenty minutes since any of us had paid attention to baseball, as far as I could tell. Chris, however, interrupted himself in mid-sentence, turned to his friend and said, "It's 7–3 Mets, bottom of the sixth, men on first and third, two outs."

Perhaps Chris is just lucky enough to be born one of the 2% of humans who are fabulous mulitaskers or "super-taskers," and the rest of us never will approach his competence. (Huge amounts of research have come out in the last decade or so revealing that except for that small minority, most of us are terrible multitaskers. Please do not use your cell phone—even hands-free—while driving [Horrey & Wickens, 2006].) But regardless of innate ability, I know that Chris practiced tracking dual conversations, offers in his environment, and emotion and intention in his scene work six times a week on stage as an improviser. He took seriously maintaining and strengthening this kind of hyperawareness. It showed in his work, and because we, his students, aspired to match his listening skills, it showed in our work as well.

We pick up information both consciously and unconsciously. Increasing listening and awareness skills is less about sensing more things and more about sensing things more consciously. At any given moment there are events and facts that we are paying attention to and a whole host of other details that are in our broader, less-conscious awareness. What the best improvisers are able to do is widen their circle of consciousness to include more information.

The great West Coast improviser, Stephen Kearin (one of the SIMS video game voices, among other things), attends to astonishingly specific details when he works. It makes him the Michael Jordan of creating vivid imaginary objects and environments. Once Kearin was teaching a class on making vocal sound effects. In one scene, a student, lying on the floor, pretended to saw off his leg. He attempted the sound of a chain saw, and Stephen stopped him. "All right," he said, "your sound is generally okay, but what are you cutting?"

The student replied, "Uh . . . my leg."

"Yeah, all right, but, listen," Stephen continued. He then performed his version of the sound, changing it subtly three or four times as he drew the imaginary blade through his limb. "Did you hear it as it cut through?" he asked. "Not just 'leg.' Flesh, bone, flesh, floor."

The lesson of Stephen's admittedly gory demonstration was that it is not the dexterity of an improviser's mouth, but the specificity of his awareness that elevates him to greatness.

Developing our awareness consists not only of increasing our capacity for information, but in heightening our awareness of the different types of information that can be gleaned.

In the "Story Exchange," a few different types of mistakes occur when participants retell the stories. The most straightforward is that facts and events get changed or dropped. Another error involves emotional content or attitude. Whereas the first storyteller might feel excited and positive, the person repeating it might express confusion or apathy. Finally, participants misconstrue the intent of the stories they hear. In other words, there are three things that we can listen for when we listen:

- Facts

- Feelings

- Intentions

Facts are the simplest to perceive. They are objective and concrete. Not that we always get them right by any means. Improvisers notoriously struggle to remember the character names they have given each other. Some improv companies have gone so far as to implement a rule that mandates everyone go by their real name on stage. Still, although we may fail to remember these details, they are ultimately black and white, right or wrong, easy to track. Improving our ability to perceive and retain facts entails simply strengthening our focus and memory. (Or finding supporting technologies, like pencil and paper to capture them. This is where note-taking and so on can be most useful in real life.)

Perceiving feelings is a little trickier. Especially in business settings, we are taught to hide and ignore our feelings. We are not used to focusing on emotions, except in the safest and most intimate environments. However, the feelings of the communicator may be more important than the specific facts. Here is an example of how the emotional content of a story got missed during "Story Exchange."

Stacey, a woman in her late twenties, described how, as freshmen in college, she and her roommate had heard a spot on the radio advertising fur coats for "$39.99." They gleefully headed to the store to pick out their coats, expecting a small, seedy storefront—but, hey, they were in college, seediness was part of the fun. When they arrived, the store was luxurious. Rows and rows of beautiful minks and foxes, sables and chinchilla hung on racks of brass. Saleswomen waited on the girls like royal servants, and when Stacey and her friend had picked out their coats, the saleswomen offered them wine in celebration, asking "Will that be cash or charge?"

The girls figured they could pay cash—even with tax the tab couldn't come to more than 50 bucks. They said so, pulling out their bills. The saleswomen went pale. "Ahem. No," they said, "the coats are three THOUSAND, nine hundred and ninety-nine dollars. Not thirty-nine dollars. These are REAL fur coats, you know." And so the girls left without their garments.

In the original telling, Stacey expressed deep embarrassment. Later, she confirmed that she remembered this incident as one of the most humiliating of her life. By the time the story got to the fourth storyteller, though, it was a story of teenage mischief. "Two hip, young college chicks set out to torture the evil fur-hocking sales ladies." Interestingly, most of the factual details stayed the same. It was the tone of the voice, the emphasis, and the look in the teller's eye that changed.

Sometimes, the details of a story are just conduits for expressing emotional content. How many of us have said things like, "You always interrupt me," or "Why don't you ever include me in meetings?" Just as many of us have had someone respond to us by saying, "I don't ALWAYS interrupt you." In these cases, it is the feeling, not the detail that it is important to hear. Unless the emotional content is addressed, all the data in the world will not result in clear communication. That is not to say that data is unimportant. If you are building a rocket ship, the specific numbers matter. In most of our communications, though, facts are just one aspect of the message. A body of work on emotional intelligence, popularized most by Daniel Goleman, tells us that our EQ (emotional quotient) correlates more strongly with success than our IQ (Goleman, 1996). Among other measures of emotional intelligence, our ability to recognize feelings and empathize deeply affects our ability to build relationships, solve problems, and influence others.

This brings us to the third kind of information we can listen for: the *intention* of the communication. Understanding the point of a message qualifies as the most important aspect of listening. To put it in terms of our discussions so far, at any given moment we are accepting a huge number of offers and ignoring others. A good listener's job is twofold: to expand the amount of information that she can take in and then quickly assess the relative value of that information. In order to understand the point of a story, we need to be able to evaluate what data is crucial and what is peripheral.

At Freestyle Rep, I had a colleague—let's call her Kelly—who was infamous for missing the most valuable pieces of information, while accepting some other innocuous offer. I remember a scene in which she played an old dowager. Her partner entered the scene as her butler. He was carrying a tray, and, as he spoke, he set the dishes and pot on the table in front of her.

"Madam," he said, "I must inform you that your son has just returned from the war. He is alive, although it looks as though he is missing a number of limbs."

"Ooh," Kelly cooed in response, "Tea! Yummy."

The actor playing the butler accepted this offer as an indication that Kelly's character was a little batty. (Remember, it is impossible to be blocked.) But the fact that it was teatime certainly was not the richest offer put forth in the scene.

In *Jump Start Your Brain*, Doug Hall and David Wecker (1995) suggest that the greatest fallacy about creativity is that material is manufactured whole cloth inside one's head. In fact, he says, the best way to create is to stimulate your imagination from the outside by dumping as much external content into your brain as possible and letting it serve as the raw stuff from which ideas are formed—rather like feeding threads into a loom or car parts onto an assembly line. Barbara Scott of BATS Improv is heralded by her fellow improvisers for her ability to receive and understand their offers. Barbara says that she has become skilled at this because she cannot come up with ideas of her own. She is being modest, but the resulting principle is valuable: Enhancing our listening and awareness abilities can increase not only communication but also creativity. Here are some non-game-based activities that you can try to enhance awareness:

- Eavesdrop on conversations.

- Mimic personalities on TV.

- Pay attention to the details of habitual activities (e.g., brushing your teeth, washing dishes, petting the dog). Turn 90 degrees and try to recreate these activities in space with imaginary objects.

- Close your eyes and quiz yourself on the details of the room you are in, your partner's clothing, your kitchen sink.

- Watch strangers and make up stories about what their lives are like, based on behaviors you observe.

- When someone tells you a story, feed back your interpretation of his or her point.

To improve their abilities to perceive facts, feelings, and intentions, actors practice "being in the moment," which means heightening one's awareness of what is happening right now. With all of our inner voices, and external pressures, being in the moment demands great discipline.

Here is the other side of the story. A model designed and researched by Ralph Nichols that suggests people's ability to listen over time maps something like this:

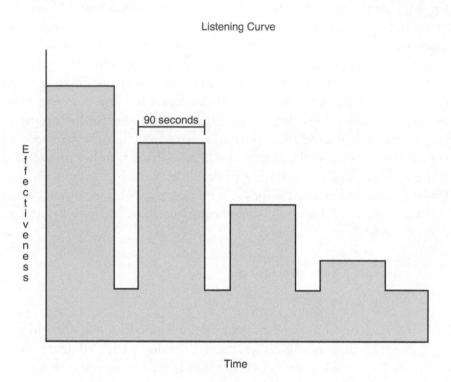

People are able to pay attention for a given amount of time, but then some word or other concern captures their attention, and they drift off. When they refocus, a gap exists in what they have heard. This means they are listening at a lower level of efficiency. There are two facts that make this reality especially discouraging.

1. Studies have shown that the amount of time people can concentrate is about 90 seconds. (And that was in 1964. These days, advertisers believe the time frame is more like 6–8 seconds.)
2. The smarter the listener is, the more quickly their listening degenerates, because more intelligent people tend to make faster and more frequent connections and, therefore, have their minds spin off on tangents more easily.

Given these realities, how can we ever communicate effectively? Improvisers know that their partner will be distracted sometimes. For goodness' sake, there are scores of people staring at them and an imaginary environment to keep track of. Therefore, in addition to practicing awareness skills, improvisers practice communicating clearly so that the information they are relating will be easier to receive. They train themselves to repeat information—like a character's name—over and over. They also learn to state their intentions clearly so that a partner does not have to struggle to discern them.

When students begin improvising, they resist explicitly voicing their intentions. The practice seems unnatural or too obvious. The most experienced improvisers, on the other hand, articulate their feelings and intentions blatantly. Strangely enough, audiences never seem to mind. Or even notice. An improviser will say, "Happy Birthday. Here's a present for you. It's a puppy," and the audience will be astonished when another improviser thinks to jump out of the box—an imaginary one, remember—as a puppy. "Oh, that was so creative," they will say of the second actor.

I was sold on the power of blatantly articulating intentions onstage, when I was picked as a volunteer during the show *Fool Moon*. The performers in the show, Bill Irwin and David Shiner, are brilliant clowns, who perform an involved first-date scene with an audience member. In this case, me. Neither of them speaks in the show, but while I was on stage, they were talking to me the whole time. "How are you feeling? You're doing great! OK, look over there. When I ask you to kiss me, say 'no'." Each step of the way they coached me, in voices easy to hear and understand. Here's the amazing part. No one noticed! Not even my date. At intermission, everyone came up to me, convinced that I must have been a plant. How could I have known what to do? How could I have supported them so well?

In a way, the audience members were right. I was not acting naturally, following my own impulses and making my own choices. But I had not been briefed ahead of time. I was briefed on stage, in the moment, in front of everyone. When I told my date that Irwin and Shiner had been speaking to me, he was shocked. He had not seen or heard a thing.

A common sales technique illustrates the power of straightforward communication in proposals for potential customers. Before presenting design ideas, skilled proposal writers include a section called some version of "Our Understanding," which summarizes the client's needs and objectives. When I first began writing proposals, I interpreted the client's concerns in my own words. I had to sound intelligent, right? I could not just parrot what they had told me. Now, I do just that. I repeat their words as exactly as I can. And the clients are delighted. I have had at least half a dozen of them tell me that it was my insightful analysis of their needs that sold them.

There is a final piece to this puzzle. No matter how much time we spend dissecting and heightening awareness, there is an unidentifiable component to it. Del Close and Charna Halpern talk about "group mind," saying:

> People who have never experienced it may be skeptical, dismissing it as New Age nonsense, but the group mind is a very real phenomenon. This is not to say that each person can read the others' minds or project specific thoughts; but when a group mind is achieved, its members have a very strong sense of the group as an entity of its own, and connect with its feelings and requirements. (Halpern, Close, & Johnson, 1994, p. 92)

"Group Counting" (page 170) illustrates this intangible connection that individuals can form with one another. The group stands in a circle and focuses on a spot or object in the center of the floor. The goal is to count "one, two, three . . ." and so on, with each successive number supplied by one and only one of the group members. The trick is that there is no order in which the participants say a number and no patterns or signals allowed. Each member of the group is required to feel when it is his or her turn to contribute a number. If more than one person offers a number at the same time, the group begins again from "one."

"Group Counting" comes as close to magic as any of the exercises I know. When I first discovered it, I thought, "Well, sure, the odds say that if they try long enough, eventually people should be able to count to 20. What's the big deal?" Very quickly, though, I realized that the activity could not be explained away that easily. My students counted to higher and higher numbers each week. By the end of a six-week session, it was not unusual to have groups counting to 70, 80, or 100 on the first or second try. That's not statistics. There are straightforward lessons that groups learn through this exercise. Things like if there are 15 people in a group, and you are counting to 20, each person, on average, gets to say only one or two numbers. If you have 22 people, two of them, at least, must remain silent. And those people who do refrain from saying a number will contribute just as much to the achievement of the goal as those who speak.

The lesson with most impact remains for me the power of our instinctual awareness of others and how quickly we can grow and harness it.

## The Principle in Action

As a trainer, it does not matter how much you know if you cannot communicate with your students. Leaders who are unable to gather and interpret information will find themselves at a significant disadvantage. Here are some areas on which to focus.

### Enhance Your Own Skills

All of the activities suggested in this chapter are recommended for the trainer or leader himself, as well as for his group. Trainers must be able to assess what their students understand, how they are feeling, what confusions they are trying to express. Just like performing, training requires a person to take in a large amount of information, even as he is presenting. In order to be successful, a trainer must have highly honed awareness skills.

I knew a trainer who had a brilliant mind and, in theory, designed terrific courses. In practice, he often lost his students, because he got so involved in presenting his material that he failed to notice when they were tired or perplexed. Participants would shift in their chairs, whisper to each other, or fall asleep, and Joe would continue on. At that point, he might as well have been presenting to stuffed dummies.

Similarly, a manager that I worked with would consistently answer a different question from the one she had been asked. She was so sure of her answers that she anticipated the question without taking time to absorb the heart of it. Questions are little flags that signal unmet needs. If we cannot effectively hear and understand them, we will miss opportunities to satisfy them.

## Read Between the Lines

Not all communication will be straightforward. Sometimes individuals will hide information intentionally. Other times they, themselves, might be unaware of their real message. Do not be satisfied with a cursory understanding of what people tell you. Look for discontinuities between the words they use and the feelings they express nonverbally. Search for the reason that someone has taken an action or made a statement. If a student asks you to repeat something, they might not have heard you. Or they might not understand the principle. Or they might disagree. If the impetus for asking was either of the second reasons, merely repeating your statement will not help. Often you will find clues in the way the question is asked or the answer is received that will let you know if you have provided a solution.

By the way, this attitude can be useful in real life, too. A friend of mine was in a relationship that ended, she said, when she and her boyfriend started taking what the other said at face value. They both ended up feeling misunderstood and uncared about.

## Train the Team

Because we have been listening since the day we were born (if not before), we do not think of listening as a skill that needs to be developed. The simple act of discussing the pitfalls and techniques of listening can improve a team's effectiveness. By also engaging in listening activities, teams can augment their listening skills and also learn more about each other. As therapists know, tenacious conflicts can disappear as soon as individuals feel they have been heard.

Listening exercises also serve as warm-up activities. Before asking participants to take in new information, remind them what skills doing so entails.

## Check for Understanding

No matter how vigilantly we try to pay attention, we will misunderstand. There is just too much information coming through too many of our own filters for us to receive messages 100% accurately. Remember Dr. Crick's quote? "80% of what we perceive to be true, we make up." Check your understanding.

## Separate Observable Behaviors From Interpretations

As coaches, we need to be adept at assessing performance and giving feedback. As we do, we must remember that objective reality is not the same as our interpretations. Listening for intentions and reading between the lines are useful, as we have said. However, remember to distinguish interpretation from the objective, observable behaviors that led to them. And when you speak to someone you are coaching, make sure to ground your assumptions in those behaviors. The individual being coached is likelier to accept and benefit from feedback when it is articulated this way. (Chris Argyris's "Ladder of Inference" in *Overcoming Organizational Defenses* [1990] and Peter Senge's Left-Hand Column work in *The Fifth Discipline* [1990] are some great tools for exploring this topic.)

Let's take the example of Gail, a manager whom a colleague of mine, Susan, was coaching. The manager struck Susan as arrogant and rather petulant. That was her interpretation. Gail's actual behaviors were rolling her eyes when Susan offered suggestions and telling Susan that her ideas would never work. Gail told stories about how lazy and belligerent her workers were and said that if it were not for her hard work, nothing would ever get done. When addressing Gail's attitude, rather than beginning with her own assumptions, Susan began by listing Gail's actions—concrete behaviors that Susan had seen and heard. Then Susan asked Gail to explain her intentions and interpretations of those behaviors. As it turned out, Gail had replaced a very popular manager and felt that her staff did not like her. Her intention was to protect herself in the face of antagonistic coworkers. After their conversation, Susan was better able to address Gail's problems, and Gail was more willing to listen.

## Articulate Your Intentions

Just as we make assumptions about others, they make assumptions about us. And the more power you have, the more others will analyze and interpret your behaviors. When someone has power over us, we scrutinize the smallest behaviors for clues to that person's thoughts and feelings. In order to avoid incorrect and potentially damaging attributions toward you as a leader, err on the side of articulating why you are doing whatever you do. Explain how you reached decisions. Share the thoughts behind particular activities and instructional designs. Frame your questions so that people do not feel attacked. It is unrealistic to expect that others will understand us all the time. The more straightforward and complete your communication, the more effective and pleasant your interactions will be.

## Feed Creativity

As we become more aware, we will find our creativity increasingly stimulated. Continue to provide sensory input to trigger creative thinking through quotes, physical objects, music, colors, and stories. Awareness is not just hard work, it is also glorious fun.

## ☞ **Key Points** ☜

- Before an offer can be accepted, it must be recognized.

- Listening is more complex than we think.

- There are three types of information to listen/watch for: facts, feelings, and intentions.

- Enhancing awareness entails making more of our unconscious processes conscious.

- Once information is received it must be analyzed and prioritized.

- Receiving information stimulates creativity.

- Enhance awareness through practice.

- Make it easier for others to listen to you by articulating your desires blatantly.

- Enhance your skills.

- Read between the lines.

- Train the team.

- Check for understanding.

- Separate observable behaviors from interpretations.

- Articulate your intentions.

- Feed creativity.

# 6
# STORYTELLING

"Our knowledge of the world is more or less equivalent to the set of experiences that we have had, but our communication is limited by the number of stories we know to tell. . . . Storytelling and understanding are functionally the same thing."
—Roger C. Schank, *Tell Me a Story*, 1995

"God made man, because he loves stories."
—Elie Wiesel, *The Gates of the Forest*, 1966

In the innocent, bygone days of 1999, a gaggle of consultants found themselves in Paris, delivering a sales course for more than a hundred participants from all over Europe. As the participants went off to prepare for their afternoon role plays, the trainers, I among them, gathered in the back of the room. Somehow a discussion of improvisational storytelling techniques began. We shared various storytelling activities and moved on to an increasingly enthusiastic exploration of their use in training situations. Our ideas for application ranged from capturing participants' attention to assessing needs to increasing retention to enhancing teamwork to reducing conflict and solving problems. By the time our training participants finished their task, we had decided that story was the foundation of all learning and communication, and the seeds for StoryNet LLC, my first consulting company, had been sown.

We were incredibly proud of ourselves. What geniuses we were to realize the profound value of storytelling. Of course, we were not alone in our assessment. Storytelling is an age-old method of communicating. From the bonfire gatherings of cavemen through the Ancient Greeks to modern times, stories have formed the foundation of our historical and cultural awareness.

In the intervening decade, storytelling has become a widely popular tool in corporate America. *Harvard Business Review*; *Fast Company Magazine*; and dozens of books including Stephen Denning's seminal *Springboard* (2001), *The Story Factor* by Annette Simmons and Doug Lipman (2006), *Tell Me a Story* by Roger C. Schank (1995), *Tales for Trainers* by Margaret Parkin (1998), and *Managing by Storying Around* by David Armstrong (1992) advocate the immense value of stories to aid communication and learning. Consultancies and professional organizations, such as Michael Margolis's Get Storied (www.get storied.com), examine story application in ways significantly more comprehensive and profound than our little group of idealistic trainers could have dreamed back in the day.

Organizational leaders now routinely turn to storytelling to develop effective branding strategies, build cultural norms, and capture organizational knowledge, as well as teaching storytelling skills to develop individuals' general communication and ability to influence others.

Why? Stories engage us more deeply and completely than presentations of mere facts without context. Our emotions are triggered, associations are stimulated, and memories are activated when we are told a story. That is why politicians have such success with anecdotes. The guy with the sweet story beats the guy with the accurate facts more often than not. On a fundamental level, Jerome Bruner, noted cognitive psychologist and learning expert, says, "Story IS meaning" (*Acts of Meaning*, 1990, p. 43). He believes that our brains are making stories all the time, taking bits of data and weaving them into meaning. Explicit storytelling satisfies us because our brains are attempting to make meaning all the time. And if the teller can provide context, intention, and coherence for us, we have received a gift. Often, we think of story as the opposite of facts and data. But, in fact, when looked at in this light, data only exists as the building blocks of narratives that we create. If a marketing manager puts up a sales graph, she is presenting a story. By learning to interpret and articulate the meaning in that graph explicitly, the speaker ensures that the story being received is the one she wanted to impart. The question becomes not, "Should we tell stories?"

but "What stories do we want to tell? And how?" David Armstrong, the vice president of Armstrong International, believed so strongly in the power of storytelling as a management tool that he incorporated it into every aspect of his family's business and eventually completely replaced the policy manual with a compilation of stories he had gathered. In the foreword to Armstrong's book *Managing by Storying Around*, Tom Peters says,

> The wild and woolly marketplace is demanding that we burn the policy manuals and knock off the incessant memo writing; there's just no time for it. It's also demanding that we empower people—everyone—to constantly take initiatives. And it turns out that stories are a—if not the—leadership answer to both issues. (1992, p. xv)

So what do improvisers have to bring to this table? Story, of course, lies at the heart of the theater's power to entertain, move, and provide catharsis. Audiences get to love, fight, grow old, die, and sing through the journeys of the characters that they watch. So as theater professionals, improvisers take the ability to create and tell good stories very seriously.

And, because improvisers, by definition, create new and fresh stories each time they take the stage, they have a special perspective on story crafting and storytelling. Whereas many storytelling books and coaching focus on having a few, "perfect" stories, improvisers focus on developing storytelling *skills*. We want to be able to tell a well-structured, compelling, meaningful, and different story every time—a story uniquely suited to the moment and the audience in front of us.

What is more, improvisers believe that because of the ancient, organic, and pervasive nature of storytelling, storytelling training comes down to making the unconscious processes that we already employ conscious. Simply put, we believe EVERYONE is a storyteller, and everyone can become a good one. Johnstone says, "It must be obvious that when someone insists that they 'can't think up a story,' they really mean that they 'won't think up a story' (1979, p. 116)." The following are some of the skills improvisers advocate and practice.

# Story Skill 1: Pay Attention

Good storytellers are good observers. They see and hear offers that the rest of us miss. By noticing and tracking details, a storyteller receives the raw material that allows them to have insight and communicate it in vivid ways. Whereas most of us might go to the DMV, for example, and stand in line impatient, bored, distracted, and then leave grumbling about the waste of time, a good storyteller will depart with a treasure of new narratives. She will have gathered information about the people around her—how they look, what they care about, why they are there. She will have noticed the falling ceiling tiles and the blinking florescent lights, the bickering between the vapid, new young clerk and the seasoned, hoary one. It will not be a coincidence that she has her colleagues spellbound and laughing as she recounts her tedious encounter the next day.

Paying attention does not just give us grist for our entertainment mill. Storytelling increases understanding—not just for the listener, but for the creator. By paying more attention to what is going on around us, we can gather more information about the who, what, why, and how of our lives. And by doing so, we expand our ability to assess situations and solve problems. Our understanding and analysis all hangs on how rich our data is. When we pay more attention, we may tell different stories, not just more or more entertaining ones. Perhaps our DMV patron, rather than telling the clichéd story of being a victim of idiot bureaucracy, comes home with a story about how the clerk helped a nervous first-time driver. Or how the supervisor got around some Kafka-esque regulation to solve a problem. Or how the guy in front of her planned to propose to his girlfriend that night. Perhaps the leader who pays attention will come up with more nuanced understandings of his people and issues as well.

# Story Skill 2: Make Connections

The quality that differentiates a story from a mere sequence of unrelated events is meaningful connection. Any data—quarterly returns, a breakdown in the supply chain, an interpersonal conflict, a design problem, a comment—begins to have meaning only when it is given context.

Improvisers know that even the most innocuous offers can become
seeds of delight when they are revisited in the narrative at a later time.
We call this *reincorporation*, and the best storytellers are masters of it.

The next time you go to a movie, pay close attention to the first
twenty minutes or so. Make note of the cutaway shots—the shots, not
of people, but of objects or scenery. Chances are that if there is a cutaway shot of an object that seems unrelated to the action in the
moment, that object will be important later on. I became conscious of
how obvious these plants are after a screenwriter friend and I went
to see *What Lies Beneath*, a standard, rather pedestrian, supernatural
thriller, starring Michelle Pfeiffer and Harrison Ford. At one point early
on, the two of them are driving across a country bridge, on the way to
a party. Ford's character decides to check messages on his cell phone.
He cannot get through, and Pfeiffer says, "Oh, you can't get a signal
while you are on the bridge." My friend turned to me and said, "Someone's gonna be trying to call for help while crossing this bridge. . . ."
Sure enough, 90 minutes later, Pfeiffer was screaming into a dead
phone, racing for the other side of the river.

Filmmakers, of course, know how the movie will end and can plant
foreshadowing events. Improvisers, because they do not know how the
scene will end, need to make whatever they set up at the beginning
important after the fact. Paul Zuckerman of Chicago City Limits calls
this driving by looking in your rearview mirror. Reincorporating is foreshadowing in reverse. From the audience, the results look like magic.
*How did they know to do that thing with the cell phone?!* an improv
audience will think.

In real life, sometimes good storytellers act as screenwriters, carefully crafting a complete narrative, planting offers at the top to rein-
corporate later on. Sometimes, however, good storytellers act as
improvisers. Either way, the principle of reincorporation proves a nifty
tool: Whatever you set up in the beginning, you bring back at the end.
As playwright Anton Chekhov reportedly put it, "If you show a gun in
Act I, it had better go off in Act III."

If, for example, a speaker incorporates details from a previous
speaker, or from a conversation with an audience member, into her talk,
all of a sudden a potentially rote speech becomes fresh and relevant.

The audience says, "Ah! She is listening, she is present." And the listeners are aided in making connections (read: meaning) that they might otherwise have missed. A leader who references a comment someone else made earlier in a meeting, or a sales person who articulates value by using an example the client shared earlier, wins trust and deepens commitment.

Here is an activity to practice integrating unanticipated offers into a narrative. Your task is to incorporate three random, unrelated words into a narrative. Here are your three words: *book*, *marmalade*, and *leap*. (Coming up with three unrelated words taxes the mind at least as much as creating a story, by the way. Another Johnstonian exercise asks pairs of improvisers to trade off back and forth, stating unrelated words until someone notices a connection. The game almost never goes more than four or five words before some relationship is evident.) Now, make up a story. You have 60 seconds. Go.

Here is what I came up with. (The following is an unedited transcription of the story I improvised.)

*Once upon a time there was a bear who loved two things: **books** and **marmalade**. Every day he would sit curled up in bed with his Big Book of Stories on his lap, and his paw in a jar of sweet and sticky orange marmalade. He never went anywhere. He didn't need to. His books transported him to far off places of intrigue and romance, while at the same time, his bed allowed him to feel safe and warm, and the marmalade sated his hunger and stimulated his senses. One day, however, something terrible happened. The marmalade from his paw had, after constant flipping of the pages, made them so sticky that they were impossible to part. The book became impossible to open. The bear panicked. What would he do now? Should he get up? No, he thought, he was too comfortable. And for a while he sat there sucking marmalade and staring out the window. Without the stories, though, to occupy his mind, he grew bored. He looked out the window and saw other bears in the distance. "I wonder what they're doing out there." The bed was still safe, and the marmalade still sweet, so he stayed, but soon the marmalade disappeared—without the book to distract him, he ate it up fast. With no stories and no marmalade, there was no choice. As scary as it was, the little bear made the **leap**. He left his bed and headed out* *into the world to find new adventure, new sweetness, and whatever else might be in store.*

How did it go for you? Was it easier than you expected? More difficult? Where did you get stuck? Were you aware of censoring yourself? What rules did you make up? What surprised you? Wasn't it satisfying to hear the words reincorporated? How did you decide what should happen next?

## Story Skill 3: Find the Game

Del Close builds on simple reincorporation by talking about the "Game" of the scene. Any of you who have children will know that patterns can be captivating. A child will play peek-a-boo for hours.

A strong crowd-pleasing scene at BATS Improv with the aforementioned Stephen Kearin illustrates finding a "game." The scene began with Stephen lying on the floor, clearly in pain, but putting on a brave face and saying to two others, "Now, kids, no more practical jokes." The rest of the scene became a series of increasingly outrageous practical jokes played by the kids on the father, culminating in the explosion of the family dog. The audience went wilder with each successive repetition of the pattern. The pattern went like this:

The father says, "Ahh, ow! Grr. Don't do that, again, kids."

The children say, "Yes, Daddy, sorry."

"OK. You're forgiven," says Dad. "I'll just go over here and . . . Oops! AAAh. . . ."

That was it. Over and over again. People ate it up. We love patterns.

In a business presentation, the "game" might take the form of a metaphor or theme that is carried throughout. "Achieving our goal will be like climbing a mountain. . . . Here are the tools we'll need to reach the summit. . . . If we don't work as a team, one of us could plummet to the rocks beneath." Or the game could be a specific format for a presentation. Astrid Klein and Mark Dytham of Klein Dytham architecture created a format called PetchaKutcha, in which all the presentations must be exactly 20 PowerPoint slides, none of which can be shown for more than 20 seconds. The International Society for Performance Improvement (ISPI) often opens its conference with a night of 99-second presentations. Sometimes the game takes the form of some kind of audience interaction—perhaps literally a game like *Jeopardy!*, or *Family Feud* with business content. Sometimes the game can be a call-and-response with an audience or telling your story through questions.

Thinking about the "game" of a story or presentation can increase the entertainment value and engagement levels, as well as aiding retention and understanding. Repetition lies at the heart of learning, and games (patterns) allow repetition to be fun.

## Story Skill 4: Structure Events

Some of you may have been thinking: Okay, yeah, anything that is connected can be considered a story, but what about that whole beginning, middle, end thing? Good point. Let's take a look at how improvisers think about creating narratives that "go somewhere." Because they are looking to tell new and fresh stories every time, and because they are often creating stories collaboratively, improvisers have broken down the story structure into some very simple and ubiquitously useful models. By mastering the fundamental principles of structuring a story, a leader or trainer can not only craft more compelling and clear stories in advance, but learn to create well-made, meaningful narratives in the moment. How valuable is that when fielding questions from confused participants or hungry media types?

The first and simplest way of looking at story structure is to simply ask the question: What should happen next? This question, "What comes next?" is the definition of *narrative action*. Johnstone turns this straightforward question into a game. One actor behaves as the puppet, and other improvisers tell her what to do. She asks, "What comes first?"

They tell her. "You pick up a newspaper.

She does, and says, "What comes next?"

"You see a picture of your long-lost husband." She does.

"What comes next?" she asks.

"You read the story next to it, which says he was discovered on a desert island."

"What comes next?"

"The doorbell rings."

"What comes next?"

"You answer the door."

"What comes next?"

"Your husband is standing there."

And so on.

An activity as simple as this can help us, as nonperformers, with our critical thinking, instructional design, and problem-solving skills. Do our processes really make sense? What am I leaving out? If I am coaching someone, do the steps I am suggesting flow logically and directly from each other? How can I make sure I am putting one foot in front of the other, doing the next most obvious and useful thing? All processes can be thought of as simple stories, and many organizations use storytelling in this way to capture best practices and transfer information.

At a slightly more complex level, a story can be said to result from establishing a routine and then breaking it. Johnstone explains this in terms of establishing "platforms" or boring, familiar situations, and then introducing a "tilt" or surprising shift. Del Close and Charna Halpern talk about setting up a relationship and an environment and then introducing some kind of "event" that changes the status quo. Although the language is different, the concept is the same. It is this establishing of routine and then breaking it that initiates any story: A small, timid Hobbit happily celebrates his uncle's birthday and hangs in the Shire as he always has. Then one day (bump bum) he gets tapped for a harrowing journey to destroy a magical ring and save the world. An inveterate bachelor enjoys a carefree existence, until he inherits a baby. A company has a corner on the phone market, until a new touch screen technology hits the scene. A longtime employee knows exactly how to do her job and gets along with all her colleagues, until she is promoted to manager. By knowing what it is that breaks the routine in your narrative, you are well on the way to having a well-structured story.

## The Story Spine

At Freestyle Rep, Kenn Adams explored the nature of story structure even more fully. Through his work in creating full-length narratives, Adams developed a number of tools to help improvisers build well-made (in the classic sense) stories. Among his tools is a template that we dubbed "The Story Spine." It has come to be valued not only by improvisers, but by keynote speakers, CEOs, advertising departments, marketers, salespeople, screenwriters, and trainers worldwide. It is by far our most popular tool, and it goes like this:

*Once upon a time* . . .

*Every day* . . .

*But one day* . . .

*Because of that* . . .

*Because of that* . . .

*Because of that* . . . *(Repeat as needed)*

*Until finally* . . .

*Ever since then* . . .

*(And the moral of the story is* . . .*)*

This template builds in a platform, a change and consequences, and a resolution. Virtually all stories, at least in Western culture, possess this structure. When a story does not fulfill this model, we feel unsettled. Sometimes the storyteller deliberately skips a piece—like leaving a chord progression unresolved—to create tension and provoke thought.

Sometimes, pieces are left out unintentionally, and we are left unsatisfied. Either way, if the storyteller does not complete the structure, the listener, in his own mind, will. (Americans are especially fond of stories that straightforwardly fulfill the Story Spine structure. Compare the French film *La Femme Nikita* with the American remake, *Point of No Return*. The second follows the structure much more rigidly, whereas the French version leaves some narrative connections ambiguous. The most glaring example of this appears about a third of the way through the film, when Nikita completes her first assignment. In the French version, she delivers room service and walks away having no idea why. In the American version, as she is leaving the premises, the building explodes behind her.)

Here is a more detailed analysis of the Story Spine, with an example of a story you might recognize, mapped into it:

*"Once upon a time . . ."*

This is the introduction to the setting and characters in the story. The platform. The exposition. It gives listeners the context and sets the stage.

Example:

"Once upon a time, in the same city, there were two prominent families who despised each other."

*"Every day . . ."*

The platform continues and develops.

Example:

"Every day the members of the family feuded, fought, and killed each other."

*"But one day . . ."*

This is the catalyst, the instigating event. This is the reason that the story is being told, the "why today is different" moment.

Example:

"But one day, the son of one of the families crashed the birthday party of the other's daughter."

*"Because of that . . ."* (Repeat at will)

This is the main body of the story; the consequences that ensue from the catalyst. Each event leads to another event, building suspense and tension.

Examples:

"Because of that, the son and daughter fell in love at first sight."

"Because of that he snuck around to her balcony and wooed her."

"Because of that, they secretly married."

"Because of that, the son did not want to kill her family."

"Because of that, he stepped into the middle of a fight and inadvertently caused the death of his best friend."

"Because of that, in agony and rage, he killed the killer, his wife's cousin."

"Because of that, he was banished."

"Because of that, the lovers needed to employ a complicated plan to be reunited."

"Because the plan was complicated and depended on other people, communication broke down."

"Because the message didn't get to him, the son didn't realize his wife was only faking her death, and he thought she was really dead when he found her in the family tomb."

*"Until finally . . ."*

Here is the climax; the clincher. The moment for which we all wait!
Example:

"Until finally he killed himself, just as the wife awoke to find her husband dead beside her, and she plunged his knife into her own body, joining her husband in death."

*"And ever since then . . ."*

The resolution. The conclusion.
Example:

"And ever since then, both families have mourned the deaths of their beloved children and stopped the nonsensical war between them."

And the moral of the story is: Feuds are stupid. Make love, not war.

Adams builds a complete structure to guide the storyteller through the different elements of a plot. Improvisers internalize the template in order to track where they are in a story and what kind of offers are needed to keep the narrative on track and satisfying.

The story spine highlights a valuable aspect of story as a communication and problem-solving tool. When our stories are clear and cohesive, then our message is too. Good storytellers keep the POINT of the story in mind. Then they decide where to start, where to end, and what the steps of that journey are in service of that point. It is often the case that when one's structure is messy, one's thinking is messy. The story spine provides a template for use when initially crafting a story, or for doctoring it (checking and revising it) after the initial drafting. It can also be used as a critical thinking tool, as we will discuss in our application section.

## Story Skill 5: Include Vivid Description

Of course, there is more to great storytelling than just what happens next. My retelling of *Romeo and Juliet* was okay, but it certainly did not rival Shakespeare's. Why not? As a matter of fact, why have all the versions of *Romeo and Juliet* pre- and post-Shakespeare been considered inferior to his? Some of it does in fact relate to the spine. Shakespeare did an excellent job of structuring his version. All of the events build on each other, creating the inevitable end. Ultimately, what distinguishes his version from the quick one related here, however, is not action, but description.

Shakespeare writes exquisitely beautiful language. His characters are robust, heart-wrenching, and entertaining. His environments echo and support the emotional action. We all know that Shakespeare (whoever you believe he was) qualifies as the Master of English theater. Perhaps no one will ever match his genius. But even we lowly mortals can enhance our stories through adding character and color to our narrative skeletons.

"Color/Advance" is a terrific activity for distinguishing action from description and developing descriptive skills. Originally based on a Spolin exercise, "Color/Advance" works like this: One player begins to tell a story. Periodically, a partner coaches him to "color" or describe some aspect of the story (e.g., a physical object, an emotion, an action). When the coach is satisfied, she calls, "Advance," and the storyteller continues the action of the story. Like so:

> Storyteller: "Once upon a time there was a sales manager named Stewart."
>
> Coach: "Color 'Stewart'."
>
> Storyteller: "Stewart prided himself on his extensive bow tie collection and colorful suit shirts. But as sharp as he appeared on the outside, Stewart was tired. He had been training Turbo-Pro industrial cleaning VAC salespeople for 26 of his 35 years with the company, and it seemed he understood and was appreciated by each generation just a little less. Stewart ate mostly in airports, and these days seemed to have trouble remembering what city he was in at any given moment."
>
> Coach: "Advance."
>
> Storyteller: "Every day Stewart took out his frustration on the salespeople who reported to him. He yelled at them; he overworked them; and he undermined their effectiveness."
>
> Coach: "Color 'undermining their effectiveness . . .'"
>
> Storyteller: "Stewart would go along on sales calls and interrupt his salespeople, make fun of their technique, and intervene to close the sale himself."
>
> Coach: "Advance."
>
> Storyteller: "One day, Stewart arrived at work to find a summons from the director of sales on his voice mail . . ."

And we will leave Stewart here to whatever his fate may be.

Using coloring and advancing like an improviser allows the storyteller (writer, teacher, lecturer, presenter) to scale their story and meet the needs of a specific audience. The structure of a lesson or points in a presentation might be very simple, but how they are illuminated can be very different, depending on the circumstances. For example, imagine a sales proposal on a new IT system. The structure of the story:

- Once upon a time (now) your company worked like this. . . .

- Every day you had to spend time on these outdated and time-consuming processes.

- But one day (now, we hope) you implemented our fabulous new system.

- Because of that, you were able to do X, Y, Z more efficiently.

- Because of that, you had better, more useful information with less time and effort.

- Because of that, you were able to save a significant amount of money.

- Until finally, you became the number one company in your industry.

- And ever since then, your stock price has gone through the roof.

That story presented to the CEO, in order to be effective, would probably need to color significantly different details than the story presented to the IT director. How many technical specifications should the salesperson include, for example? How much financial analysis? A sense of what details to color, and how to color them vividly and in a meaningful way, results in great stories aligned with a specific audience's needs.

## Story Skill 6: Be Flexible

There is no such thing as one right story—or one right way to tell a story. The power of a story, as we have been discussing, lies in its ability to connect with a specific audience in a specific moment and share a specific experience or message. A story that might play perfectly in one context might fall terribly flat in another. Employing all the skills we have investigated so far allows you to maximize the probability that you will be able to connect with and impact your audience.

An example: I was once hired as a keynote speaker to talk about team building. The audience was made up of the remote ticket counter personnel (the ones not located at the airport) of a major airline. For the event, I prepared all sorts of great stories and activities about collaboration and teamwork. GREAT stories. Then I arrived at the venue. I had specifically been asked not to sit in on the morning session, so I came around lunchtime, 45 minutes or so before I was scheduled to speak.

"Hi," said my contact. "We're so looking forward to your talk. Oh, and by the way, we just let everyone know that, within the next two years, we will be closing all the remote offices, and they will all be laid off."

My stories about teamwork and trust suddenly seemed less fabulous. "Oh," I replied.

I stared ahead at the throngs of eating, soon-to-be-unemployed attendees. Above the stage where I would be speaking was a banner that read, "There is no *I* in team." Ah! Thank goodness, I had gotten in the habit of collecting stories. I remembered an interview I had heard with Michael Jordan the week before. The biggest star the basketball world had ever seen had been presented with this very phrase. His reply? "Yeah, but there is in 'win.'"

So I told that story. A story with exactly the opposite point that I had been hired to relay. Everyone laughed—a huge relieved laugh. How humiliating for all of us, if I had simply stuck to my script. And perhaps most amazingly, I was then able to talk about teamwork skills: how to apply them to job interviewing; how to create opportunities for each other; how to create a supportive environment, especially in the hard times; how to find strength in solidarity. The participants knew exactly what I was talking about. And the client, by the way, was perfectly, obliviously happy.

When the disconnect between what we have planned or anticipated and the reality of the moment is less stark, it is easier to overlook. But there is a price for missing it. The next time you start to tell a story, ask yourself, "Why am I telling THIS story to THIS audience at THIS moment?" And, "Where might I want to depart from my script?"

## Story Skill 7: Build Your Library; Browse the Stacks

Storytelling is personal. In fact, that is one of the reasons thought leaders tout its value. A story, well chosen and well told, opens a window into the teller and reveals what makes him unique and complex. The same story told by two tellers can feel profoundly different. What we choose to emphasize and how we choose to perform is as individual as our DNA. What is more, we all have many stories. The old question, "What's your story?" misses the point. We are an amalgam of dozens of dozens of stories that we tell ourselves and others and that define how we and our audiences see the world.

Therefore, the more stories one gathers, crafts, and shares, the more power one has to communicate specific messages and to connect in varied ways.

I was struck by how many stories each of us has, when doing some media training with Paralympic athletes. As you may know, the Paralympic Games run parallel to the Olympic Games and allow disabled athletes the ability to compete at the same elite levels as their Olympic counterparts. Under the auspices of Performance of a Lifetime, we were working with the "ambassador" athletes on developing their personal stories. The stories were meant to introduce the athletes to the public and to promote the Paralympic organization and their programs.

You can imagine, I am sure, the intensity and drama inherent in personal stories told by any athlete who is at the top of her field and has also learned to navigate with amputated limbs or blindness or cerebral palsy. So when the stories initially struck us as deeply moving and meaningful, we were not surprised. What was surprising, though, was how quickly we seemed to become immune to some version of that story. As inspiring as the stories were (and they were *inspiring*, even though many of the athletes balk at the term), after a few iterations, they lost their full impact. It seemed the athletes fell into a habit of telling their stories in generic ways—the way they thought the story should go. In other words, we heard the mainstream, predictable Hollywood versions. Time after time, the story went something like:

- Once upon a time, I was an able-bodied elite athlete.

- Every day I engaged in strenuous, high-level athletic activity.

- But one day, I got injured.

- Because of that, I had these physical problems.

- Because of that, I got depressed and almost gave up.

- Because of that, my friend (family member, doctor) connected me with Paralympics.

- Until finally, I realized that I could still live life fully and even compete physically.

- Ever since then, I have felt happy and whole.

- And the moral is, through the Paralympic organization, you or your loved ones can discover fabulous opportunities and a new lease on life.

After just a few minutes of conversation, however, it became clear that these athletes were—of course—richly three-dimensional people, with hundreds of individual and strongly differentiated accomplishments and attitudes toward their sport and their roles as ambassadors. By rummaging just a little more deeply in the filing cabinet of their experiences, each athlete discovered something—no, many, many things—to share that proved more personal, less predictable, and, therefore, more moving, enlightening, and memorable. One example that has stuck with me was told by Sam Kavanagh, an elite cyclist who rediscovered his passion and talent for cycling after losing a leg in an avalanche while skiing with some friends. Now, as we said, this story already has plenty of drama inherent in it, but when Sam thought deeply about a message that he profoundly believed and cared about, he came up with a story smaller in scope than the one that fit the template just described. And, I think, one with even more impact. With his permission, here it is. (Of course in real life, we need not literally use the Story Spine language, but for the sake of illustration and comparison, I've recorded it in that format.)

- Once upon a time, Sam was recovering from a double amputation, after surviving a horrific skiing accident.

- Every day he sat in his living room, barely able to move. When he needed to go to the bathroom, he would drag himself there, and was so spent by the effort that he would need to rest for 45 minutes before returning to the couch.

- But one day, his wife dragged out his stationary bike and said, "Okay, it's time. Get on."

- Because of that, Sam was pissed off.

- Because of that, he said, "What the _____? Are you crazy? I can barely move. I can't ride that thing."

- Because of that, his wife said, "Get on!" They fought for a while, but she insisted, dragging a chair over to support his stump and helping him on.

- Because of that, Sam rode for two minutes or so and then nearly collapsed from exhaustion.

- Because of that, he was terribly depressed, and when his wife cheered for him, he said, "What are you talking about? I could barely do two minutes. I used to be able to ride for eight hours straight."

- Until finally, his wife replied, "Yeah? How much did you do yesterday?"

- Ever since then, Sam has remembered to appreciate the SMALL victories and accomplishments, and by committing to incremental progress, he has become a world-renowned Paralympic cyclist.

- And the moral is, "Remember to celebrate the two minutes."

Sam's message has personal meaning for him, so it has meaning for his audience. And for any audience. One need not be struggling with a lost limb or striving for athletic achievement to identify with Sam's story. This story is uniquely Sam's, and it delivers a universally useful and moving message. One we can all benefit from.

Sam's story is also flexible. When speaking to an audience who might have an injured relative, Sam focuses on a different moral—that sometimes a push is the best kind of support, for example. Sam has many other "small" stories, too. By harvesting his experiences for moments that have special meaning for him, he has become as elite a speaker as he is an athlete. (You can find out more about Sam and follow his career at nolimbitations.com.)

Leaders and trainers, too, can have more impact and build deeper relationships if they move away from simple templates of the stories they think they are supposed to tell, in favor of truly personal and specific narratives. Although knowing the "six kinds of stories every leader should have" might be helpful in theory, the power of story quickly erodes when it becomes reified or paint-by-the-numbers-y. By paying attention to yourself and your own experiences, you will discover that you have many more stories to share than you may think.

# Application

The field of storytelling in business has grown alongside the field of applied improv in recent decades. There is much too much literature and application of story in organizations to capture here. (See the beginning of this chapter for a few recommended resources.) But simply looking at the activity of formal training, we can find a plethora of useful applications. When we can make the process of narrative creation conscious, our training and organizational effectiveness skyrockets. Specifically, use stories and storytelling activities in the following ways.

## Pique Interest

Stories make the content interesting. No matter how brilliant your information is, if people are not engaged, they will not absorb it. Stories can be used to break the ice, establish credibility and empathy, or frame the intention of a policy. They can add humor, suspense, and drama. Look for opportunities to tell stories at every turn.

## Use Stories for Introductions

Another reason that stories are such a powerful communication tool is that they are dynamic. The story resides as much in the mind of the listener as in the mouth of the teller. Students become more involved in their own learning when they engage in a story—even if it is just listening to one—rather than being asked to receive rote facts. Supplying opportunities for others—learners or team members—to share their own stories has added benefits. As a form of introduction, stories communicate more personal and memorable information than mere statistics, such as title, years of experience, and objectives. In addition to telling the story of their name, as described previously, some examples of stories that participants can share include:

- Pivotal stories from their work life.

- Their most exciting adventure.

- The story of how they arrived at the workshop—starting from whenever they wish—birth, that morning, their first day at the company.

## Assess Needs

Stories can provide information about learners' expectations, previous knowledge, and applicable skills. In formal learning environments, participants themselves might not be aware of all of the intricacies of their needs and relevant experience. Through stories, you, the trainer, can gather robust and relatively complete data about learners' pedagogical and personal needs. Some specific ways to elicit this information include having participants:

- Tell the story of what they got out of the workshop at the beginning of the session, as if it were over.

- Share a true story of a great success they have had in order to gather best practices and tips to share.

- Relate a story of frustration or disappointment as a way of determining some specific objectives and challenges.

Another way to assess needs through storytelling techniques is to modify the "Color/Advance" activity described earlier. Teach the color/advance vocabulary to the group and allow people to prompt "color" or "advance" as you lecture. This enables participants to express their needs in the moment as you present.

Finally, stories need not be formally incorporated into training designs in order to provide clues to the needs of the learners. Listening to the stories people tell at breaks and probing for stories when questions come up are also excellent ways of harvesting needs. Leaders gain at least as much from soliciting stories as by sharing their own.

## Increase Retention

Because learning is innately a storytelling process, the conscious use of storytelling activities assists in the process of retention. As review activities, you might:

- Have participants—individually or in groups—create a story that illustrates a learning point or principle.

- Provide a story that illustrates a process or incorporates data as a mnemonic device.

- Have participants write the story of the workshop as a way of assessing retention and evaluating understanding.

When asking participants to create stories, Adams's Story Spine has proven to be an excellent tool. The structure works as a guide and tends to relieve whatever pressure individuals might feel to tell "good" stories. If you are asking people to work collaboratively, the Spine also helps to align the create efforts.

## Enrich Visioning and Problem Solving

Traditional visioning activities can result in beautiful pictures, but often leave the path to those Elysian fields murky. Through the use of storytelling, groups are able to flesh out the process as well as the goal. Again, the Story Spine works in this context. If the "vision" is the happy ending—the "ever since then,"—what is the story that will get us from here to there? What obstacles will be overcome? How will each team member contribute?

Another story format that can be adapted to problem-solving sessions is Joseph Campbell's The Hero's Journey. The Hero's Journey is an analysis of the ubiquitous quest structure found in works as disparate as *Star Wars*, Homer's *Odyssey*, and *Mr. Smith Goes to Washington*. A breakdown of the formula can be found in Campbell's own *The*

*Hero With a Thousand Faces* (1973), as well as in storytelling and screenwriting books, including Christopher Vogler's *The Writer's Journey* (1998). The Hero's Journey is a more specific and focused expansion of a structure like the Story Spine and includes archetypes such as the reluctant hero, the wise mentor, and the monsters, which can be useful metaphors for anyone's movement toward a new goal.

## Build Teams

Remember how bonded you felt to your camp friends? There was nothing like hanging around a campfire, singing songs and exchanging ghost stories. Somehow other relationships never felt as satisfying and intense. All the ways that we have discussed so far to improve teamwork—getting to know each other better, enhancing empathy, building on each other's ideas, listening well—live in storytelling activities. The effect is enhanced when the group creates stories together. It hardly matters what the content of the stories are. Whenever there is an opportunity to share stories or invent them collaboratively, we recommend it.

## ☞ Key Points ☜

- Storytelling is a historic, current, and profound learning tool.

- Stories are at the heart of theater and at the heart of communication.

- The difference between a list of events and a story is connectivity.

- Reincorporating is the foundation of a story.

- "What happens next?" is a fundamental question of stories.

- Stories establish a routine and then break it.

- The Story Spine defines the structure of a well-made story.

- Detail enhances the action of a story and makes it more compelling.

- Be flexible with how you tell your stories and about which stories you tell.

- Build your library. The more stories you gather, the more powerfully you can communicate your messages.

- Pique interest through stories.

- Use stories in learning environments:

    - For introductions.

    - To assess need.

    - To increase retention.

    - To enrich visioning activities.

    - To build teams.

# 7
# PERFORMING WITH PRESENCE

"It is a known fact that the human body and psychology influence each other and are in constant interplay."[25]
—Michael Chekhov, *To the Actor*, 1953

". . . the most important thing that the storyteller has to consider in nonverbal communication is that of 'congruence,' that is making sure that what you say is being backed up by what you do or how you appear."[26]
—Margaret Parkin, *Tales for Trainers*, 1998

Improvisers take on three roles whenever they step on stage. Simultaneously, they function as actors, directors, and writers. The writer-third of the improviser can easily fall into the trap of "telling not showing." As playwrights know, behavior trumps words in impact. (You know what they say about the relative value of pictures and words.) Still, because we are so much more conscious of the words we use, it is easy to forget that communication depends on so many nonverbal cues. A number of the exercises that Spolin created are silent—no words allowed—for just this reason. In one exercise, improvisers pair up to do a scene with only one person able to speak. Observers and the players alike find that the mute improviser has just as much power to make offers and further the action of the scene as the verbal one. When improvisers are forced to relinquish their language skills, they see how much they can communicate with their bodies.

There are three aspects of the nonverbal work in improv that are useful outside of the theatrical world. They are: honing a strong and supple instrument, aligning the mind and the body, and identifying status. Let's take them one by one.


## Honing the Instrument

Most artists use tools external to themselves. The painter has his brushes and canvases; the writer has her pen and paper; the musician has his keyboard, trumpet, or violin. What the actor has is herself. A significant portion of acting training is spent in movement, voice, and speech classes. The concept is that no matter how much you feel or how brilliant the words you speak are, if you do not have a strong "instrument," you will not be able to communicate the beauty of the music. Great musicians invest millions of dollars in Stradivarius violins. Actors are stuck with whatever body they are born with, and they must transform them into precious instruments.

Improvisers depend on their bodies and voices to be both strong and flexible. In the course of a two-hour show, they might play a dozen distinct characters. Each character, while looking, moving, and sounding different (all without costumes and props, mind you) must be comfortably seen and heard by the audience. That requires physical stamina and agility. The exercises designed to build those skills are straightforward. Developing a strong instrument involves ongoing conditioning and practice. Like athletes, the best improvisers work out regularly and warm up before game time.

What is true on stage is just as true when running a workshop, giving a sales presentation, or motivating a team. Your body should be relaxed and open, your voice should be audible and pleasant, and both should convey the feelings and intent behind your words.

In addition to this general conditioning, there are specific techniques that performers learn to adapt their behaviors to stage or screen. Stage actors practice projecting their voices and extending their gestures to fill unnaturally large spaces, for example. Film and television actors learn to reduce extraneous movements, because the camera will exaggerate them.

Increasingly, professionals of all kinds find they must acquire these kinds of formal performance skills. Leaders speak at annual meetings for audiences of thousands. Salespeople give presentations to clients across the world via teleconferencing technology. The pressure to present well continues to increase. The public has become acutely conditioned by television and judges as much on appearance as on substance.

Dennis Miller, the caustic comedian and HBO talk show host, has a famous rant about what fun most Americans made of Ross Perot's running mate, Admiral James Stockdale, after his appearance in the 1992 vice presidential debate. The admiral was a kind and respected intellectual with a distinguished military record. He also happened to be uncomfortable on camera. As Miller says, Stockdale committed the only unpardonable sin of our culture. He looked bad on television. In 1992, it was still possible to express shock that looking good on camera should matter so much. These days, it is a reality that we take for granted, often without a second thought.

## Aligning Mind and Body

Training the body in the ways previously discussed is relatively common in presentation and media training courses. It fundamentally consists of physical training, like working out. Although it might not always feel comfortable or easy, it is pretty straightforward.

Another, slightly more complex area of nonverbal training addresses the connection between the body and the mind. Kirk Livingston, a former artistic director of BATS Improv, told me that the most important thing he has learned in his nonverbal training is that "the body is always in the present, whereas the mind floats around in the past and the future." In other words, if we wish to be spontaneous and aware, our physical selves are the key to success. Our bodies have no choice. They must be in the moment. For the most part, they cannot whisk themselves out of the room if they feel threatened or shy. Our minds do that all the time. Our bodies cannot be in two places at once. Many of us are in three or four places at the same time mentally. What Livingston suggests then, is that our bodies are more reliable than our minds. They are more in touch with the reality around them and, therefore, they are better guides to making real connections.

As babies, we are completely integrated. When we feel a physical sensation, we cry out with deep emotion until we are comfortable again. When we are angry or sad, we scrunch up our bodies and faces and turn beet red as we cry. We sleep when we are tired, without worrying about what will happen tomorrow.

As we get older, we separate our thoughts from our immediate physical sensations. One of the ways we do this is by tensing our muscles and holding our breath to cut off the connection. That is why babies make much clearer, louder crying sounds than adults, even though they are so much smaller. But as much as we may want to separate mind and body, the two affect each other. Some of the most progressive businesses have begun to invite masseurs into the offices for just this reason. They realize that if their employees are physically comfortable and healthy, they will also feel more content and work more productively. A colleague of mine, who specializes in creative problem solving, advocates going for a walk when the solution to a problem has eluded you for a length of time. "It is easier to change your body, than to change your mind," he says.

Individuals have comfort zones, and some people feel more in touch with their physicality, some with their feelings, some with their intellects. Athletes, for example, tend to have heightened sensitivity to and control over physical experience. Computer programmers tend to depend on their mental capabilities. I am reminded of my own tendency to depend on my cerebral capacities when I interrupt my writing to perform. One night, I found myself focusing so much on my intellect—planning what I should say and analyzing the scenes I was in—that I felt sluggish and uninspired. I would have gone home completely discouraged if I had not been called upon to play a pig in one scene. As a pig, I could only communicate nonverbally. I had no words, just squeaks, and eyes, and little hooves. I was forced to be present and connected to my body. I am sure it was my most creative work of the night. Certainly the audience thought so.

Individuals in business settings tend to depend on their minds more than their bodies. Business professionals report that they spend much more time planning *what* they will say in presentations than they do practicing *how* they will say it. The world of business is extremely abstract. However, the Mehrabian study discussed in chapter 1 confirms the fact that, even in business settings, we trust vocal and visual cues much more than we do verbal cues. Again, his statistics say that when we decide whether or not to trust a message, we make our decision based on the following percentages: How the speaker looks, 55%; How she sounds, 38%; What she says, 7%. At first, workshop participants express shock at this statistic. However, it is not really that surprising. Words come from our sophisticated, conscious brains. Our physical and vocal responses emanate from much more primitive, and therefore less controlled, places.

What this truth leads us to is the realization that no matter how brilliant the content we have to deliver is, we had better get our bodies along for the ride, or we have much less power to affect and convince our audience. Casting directors say that they make their decisions about the actors who audition for them within the first fifteen seconds of their audition. They do not have to wait to hear how the monologue unfolds. They can tell from the way the actor looks, sounds, stands, moves, whether he will fulfill their requirements. Similarly, the success of a trainer, salesperson, or manager may be much more connected to how the message is delivered than we like to think.

For the same reasons that physical and vocal communication is powerful, students often confront it with discomfort and confusion. As soon as we engage our voices and bodies we become vulnerable. We must tear down the walls that have protected us. The reward we receive in exchange is an ability to affect and be affected. It is a valuable power, indeed. A number of the spontaneity and trust-building exercises in this book, double as techniques to increase physical comfort and awareness. The uneasiness that comes with the first forays into this area is more than worth the results.

A final point about the integration of the internal and external experience: It is possible to develop from the outside in, or the inside out. British acting training tends to work the first way, and American the second. Sometimes, if a student is struggling with her physicality, asking her to change her internal focus can help.

A number of years ago, a colleague and I were hired by a major software company to train their new spokeswoman. She was to be their new "human face," designed to make their image more attractive to the home consumer. "Carey" had already been exposed to media training, but she came to us nervous and confused. From her previous coach, she had learned how to sit, how to stand, what not to say. What she had not learned to do is behave authentically. During the two days that we were together, we had Carey practice telling stories from her own life and talk about her own passions and desires. As she opened up, her face and body relaxed and, without thinking, she began to look more attractive, more convincing, and easier to understand. For her, the key was internal connection, and the external behavior took care of itself.

Whether you approach integration from the inside out or the outside in, the integration remains imperative. Just as a house divided against itself cannot stand, an instrument divided against itself cannot sing.

## Status Behaviors

A more specific area of nonverbal work that is explored throughout improv communities is status behaviors. *Status*, in this context, is defined as power dynamics. Status dynamics permeate all aspects of human interaction.

Status is not the same as official title or rank, although they may connect in some ways. In studying power, social science researchers have investigated different sources of power. They have then divided them into two classes, positional and personal. We make a mistake if we assume the two always go hand in hand. The ineffectual VP may have less actual status than the efficient personal assistant. Status is both fundamental and complicated. Words, actions, clothing, title, knowledge all combine to define a person's status.

As a way of looking at relationships and dramatic action, status entered the improvisational lexicon via the work of Keith Johnstone. I do not think it is a coincidence that Johnstone, a Brit, focused on the concept when none of his American counterparts did. In the United States, we eschew the concept of class and power. Everyone is supposed to be created equal, and so that must mean everyone is equal. An awareness of status differences, especially within a small community or team, has come to constitute political incorrectness. Organizations flatten their hierarchies and expect that status differentials will disappear. And perhaps not surprisingly, it is often those with the most power who resist the concept the most strongly. As social science tells us, the privileged are often blind to their privileges.

But make no mistake. Status dynamics exist. All the time, everywhere. What may distinguish one culture from another is what characteristics endow someone with status, which behaviors are expected of individuals with differing status roles, and how stable those roles are. Johnstone's genius was to recognize that status can be understood not as something we *are*, but as something we *do*.[27] We confer or accept status through our behaviors, and it is those interactions that determine who is perceived as holding the power.

Johnstone found that when his students "played" high or low status, their work on stage became richer and looked more like real-life behavior. It is his focus on behaviors that signal high or low status that has proved so useful in communication-skills training.[28] Through an exploration of these nonverbal cues, students heighten their perceptions of status relationships and learn to raise and lower their own and others' status. Peter Falk's detective character, Colombo, for example, plays low-status in order to confound murderers, who often hold high-status positions. Ultimately, Colombo wins through his tenacity, brilliance, and expertise, but in the meantime, he tricks his adversaries into underestimating him, so that they let their guards down.

Psychologists John Levine and Richard Moreland say, "Humans, like other animals, usually have little difficulty reading signs of status and recognizing who defers to whom. People high in status in a group tend to talk more and are freer to interrupt. They also display their status nonverbally, by standing erect, maintaining eye contact longer, and generally displaying signs of confidence" (2002, p. 189).

Johnstone adds, high-status individuals tend to move fluidly and hold their heads still. Low-status behaviors, he says, include making oneself small physically and vocally, saying "um . . ." and "uh . . ." a lot, touching one's face and hair, and trying to make eye contact but looking away quickly. The first set of behaviors signals calm and security; the second, nervousness and a desire to hide or please.

Playing with status highlights the power of nonverbal behaviors to change the sense of a message. In an exercise adapted from *Impro*, participants are given a short script of neutral dialogue and asked to play it over and over with different status relationships. The huge effect of a roll of the eyes or a giggle is stunning. Often, I will use a job-interview setting for the short scene, written by the students. It might look something like this:

A:  Good morning.

B:  Good morning.

A:  Have a seat.

B:  Thank you.

A:  I have looked over your resume.

B:  Yes?

A:  I see you worked at Global, Inc.

B:  Yes. For a number of years.

A:  Very impressive.

B:  Thanks.

Participants usually begin with the assumption that the interviewer will have high status by default. All the actor playing the role must do, though, is sound impressed and eager to please, and the interviewee's status rises. Conversely, even a line like "very impressive" can seem cutting when said with a dismissive tone.

Because it is so fundamental to our social structures, our sensitivity to status is highly honed. "Status Cards" (page 207) illustrates this awareness. Participants are given a playing card that they put on their foreheads without looking at the face. The card signifies their status, and the group treats each member accordingly. When they are asked to line up in order of status, based on how they were treated, most groups have more than 90% accuracy, and many individuals can guess their cards exactly.

Not only are we aware of status, but the desire for it is an exceptionally strong motivator. Keith Allred, an expert in negotiation theory, stated in one of his classes at Columbia University that people will give up tangible gains—like money—in exchange for status.[29] And, he says, they will reject agreements that are clearly within their best interests, if they feel like they are not getting the respect they deserve. It makes sense that status wields such influence in human interactions. Historically, the guy with the highest status got the best food and the most opportunities to procreate. (That is probably still true, though the attributes that confer status may have changed.)

Status is not static. You might have high status in one situation (for example, giving a presentation) and low status in another (fixing your computer). Think about your family: Who has the highest status when it comes to making decisions about money? How do you know? What behaviors does that person engage in that signal she or he has the status? How about when it comes to deciding which movie to see, or what to serve for dinner? Does the same person have the same status?

In my coworker Mandy's family, her mother has always controlled the financial aspects of her family's life. Her mother is extremely generous and not visibly controlling, but her status is clear. Mandy's father actually makes more money, but he deposits it in a joint bank account and goes to his wife when he wishes to make a major purchase. She has the power. There are a number of reasons that her mother holds this status. The main one is she loves to manage the money. Her husband doesn't care to. In this situation, he has the positional power as the breadwinner, but she has status stemming from her knowledge, expertise, and passion.

Now consider your organization. What attributes confer the most status on individuals there? Title? Expertise? Age? Gender? Knowledge? Affiliation? In which situations do you feel you have status? Are there situations in which you would like to have more? Less?

Once people recognize that status exists, they might assume that everyone craves high status all the time. However, some of us are not most comfortable in the visibly high-status role. In *Impro*, Johnstone said he believed "that people have a preferred status; that they like to be low, or high, and that they try to maneuver themselves into the preferred position" (p. 43).[30] A colleague of mine, for example, claims that she prefers to be the second in command. There is always someone else to go to for help, to learn from, and to pass the buck to. Yet, she has affiliative power and enough status to be included in important decisions and exciting activities. Where do you think you are most comfortable? What about each of your direct reports? Your trainees? Does it change with the situation?

Businesspeople and performers benefit from status awareness in contradictory ways. For the performer, knowledge of status is useful because it is the stuff of drama. Take the great Greek tragedies. They are all about a character with extremely high status—a king, a god—falling from grace. Many American classics recount the story of a low-status character attempting to achieve the American Dream—acquire money and fame and, hence, status. Improvisers study status because it helps them create drama. Changes in status make for compelling action on stage.

Trainers and leaders working in business settings find status awareness useful for the opposite reason. By learning to equalize status, they can enhance communication and motivation.

Remember the trust formula? If the status gap gets too big, people do not believe that leaders can empathize with them, so they do not feel safe. And a leader, if he is separated from his people by too big a status gap, fails to get important information and advice.

Through an awareness of status interactions, trainers can raise the status of their learners to facilitate participation and comfort. Or they can raise their own status to focus the group. Managers can set effective limits or seem more accessible. Individual contributors can increase the possibility that their ideas will be heard and valued. Salespeople can connect with their clients, children can appease their parents, and couples can resolve sticky issues that they might not have understood before. For a further discussion of the topic, consult *Impro*, or for an academic approach, look to French and Raven's seminal work on social power dynamics ("The Bases of Social Power," 1959).[31]

As we strengthen our physical and vocal instruments, align our bodies with our minds, and raise our awareness of the effects of our behaviors, we augment our communicative prowess. It is not a fluke that our political and community leaders are increasingly being drawn from the ranks of performers.

# Application

When the business community first began to turn to theater profession-als, it was for presentation-skills and media training. It is no trick to translate theatrical techniques to the performance aspects of business communication. As I am sure you have already discovered, there is more to it than that. The behavioral, vocal, and status-based exercises included in this book provide guidelines for developing skills that busi-ness professionals ignored for many years and are now learning to value and address consciously. They are suitable both as workshop activities and as personal development tools. Apply them in the following ways.

## Enhance Presentation Skills

The most straightforward application of this nonverbal work is, in fact, presentation skills. The leader explaining a strategy or setting direction, the trainer standing in front of a classroom, or the sales manager giving a report, each needs to be seen and understood and needs to inspire confidence and enthusiasm. Whenever a person presents in a formal situation, the effects of their gestures and vocal tones are magnified. A habitual gesture that might not be noticeable one-on-one can loom large on the stage. The time to think about the nonverbal aspects of a presentation is not during the presentation. There are plenty of other things to focus on then. Strengthen your voice and body ahead of time through regular exercise and spend as much time planning the form of your presentation as you do planning the content. (Form, by the way, includes not only your physical and vocal work, but also all of the "set and costume" trappings. What do your slides look like? Is your handwriting legible? What are you going to wear?)

## Align the Mind and the Body

Because the body and the mind are connected, they affect each other. This is hardly news for those of you who have lain awake at night worrying about a project or relationship. The good news is that by taking care of our bodies we can relieve stress and increase productiv-ity. During a presentation, for example, taking the time to breathe slowly and deeply can reduce nervousness as well as its physical manifestations.

A strong body can also help a trainer maintain concentration and energy throughout a session. When the body gets tired, so does the brain. An eight-hour day constitutes an awfully long performance. Even with breaks, it requires physical as well as mental stamina.

In a related vein, the more healthy and alert your body is, the more attuned you can be to the environment; and, as we know, listening and awareness enhance both creativity and communication. In addition to the external environment, your own body will give you useful data. If you feel hungry, perhaps your students do, as well. If your gut feels tense, perhaps there is some sort of conflict that you need to resolve. Take care of your body and then listen to what it tells you.

## Make Conscious Status Choices

An ability to manipulate status dynamics is a potent tool. As noted, the more equalized the status, the smoother the communication. Facilitation, mediation, negotiation, and presentation skills all depend to some degree or another on this capacity. A trainer may choose to raise the status of his students to increase their sense of control and feeling of competence, for example. This can be achieved through an action as subtle as sitting rather than standing, or one as blatant as turning over the position of teacher to a participant. A new manager may choose to change his gestures and vocal patterns to sound more confident, and therefore credible, when speaking to the CEO. A coach can pay attention to the subtle signs of high or low status in the person being coached and adjust in order to keep communication flowing.

When experimenting with status, here are a couple of tips to keep in mind. First, inauthentic behavior will be spotted and backfire. Our animal sense is keen. The power here resides in aligning behavioral signals with our intentions. If the two are not aligned, the results could be ineffective, embarrassing, or at worst, unethical.

Second, the qualities that bestow status on someone vary widely from environment to environment. What one wears in a law firm to garner high status is not the same as what one wears on a football field—or at a dot-com, for that matter. The same holds true for vocabulary, story, and pedagogical and managerial choices. Know your audience. What will they identify with? Which stylistic choices are they used to? What is their preferred status relationship?

If you are conscious, aligned, and authentic, your nonverbal behaviors can catapult your effectiveness to increasingly higher levels of mastery. Although stretching in these ways might feel unnatural at first, these ways of expanding your performance range can have deep impact.

☞ **Key Points** ☜

- Nonverbal behavior often carries more weight than the verbal communication.

- Three aspects of nonverbal behavior from theatrical work are:

    - Forging a strong body.

    - Aligning the mind and body.

    - Status.

- An actor's (or presenter's) body is his instrument.

- Giving a presentation is like being on stage.

- We focus more on content than on form, even though form is so important, because developing our voices and bodies can be uncomfortable at first.

- *Status* is defined as power dynamics.

- Status can be viewed as something we do, not something we are.

- Status is fluid and variable.

- Status comes from a variety of personal and positional criteria, including nonverbal behaviors.

- Personal and positional status positions are not always aligned.

- We are very attuned to, and motivated by, status.

- Individuals may have preferred status roles.

- The more equal the status, the more communication is facilitated.

- The more we learn to consciously shift and expand our range of performance, the more positive impact we can have.

# SECTION TWO

# Activities

Skip Downing — *On Course*

# INTRODUCTION TO THE ACTIVITIES

As I mentioned in the introduction, *Training to Imagine* does not purport to be a comprehensive compilation of improvisational theater games. There are such texts. The ones I recommend are included at the end of the book. The exercises I have included in this section are those I have found offer the most value to individuals training and working in business settings. In writing the game descriptions, I have assumed that the reader possesses a certain level of facilitation experience. My goal was to provide enough material about each activity, so that the trainer understands the flow and applications of each game. In addition to the general rules, I have included suggested tips and debrief questions. Depending on the focus of the training, different questions will apply. For more general tips on facilitating games and simulations, I recommend *Interactive Strategies* by Thiagi (2000) or his website, www.thiagi.com.

There are often a number of variations included with each exercise description. Some of these are simple modifications, whereas other variations could qualify as separate activities. I have grouped the exercises in terms of their learning points and their central techniques. As for the origins of each activity, let me reiterate: I have done my best to attribute each game accurately, though the task was made difficult by the oral nature of our art form and years of cross-pollination among improv organizations. The descriptions are my adaptations and articulations of exercises gleaned from a variety of sources. My source attributions include the actual inventors of the games in some cases, when I felt I could be relatively sure of them. When I was unable to track a game to its beginnings, I reference the individuals and organizations that introduced me to it. If you believe you have further information regarding the origins of an activity, please let us know.

Since the first publication of this text, readers and colleagues have requested further tips on choosing and facilitating activities. The following are some additional thoughts on those topics.

## Choosing Activities

In the appendix, you will find three tables. One of them sorts activities by improv topics, and the other, by general organizational development topics. A third table lists the activities new to this edition. Included in the tables is also information about group size and time needed. These are provided to streamline your search. In addition, here are some broader theoretical thoughts about choosing activities.

Actors have another little tidbit that we can steal. When preparing a scene, they ask, "What is my objective?" This simple question should be asked by anyone attempting to communicate anything. Certainly, it serves the trainer greatly.

Any interaction with another has embedded in it a desire to change another. Perhaps we want them to be changed by knowing a new piece of information (knowledge): "Turn right at the second light."

Or to affect how they feel (attitude/belief): "What a lovely dress!" "You heartless cad!"

Or to change their ability to do something (skill): "Hold the violin like this. Move your bow thusly."

When training others this intention becomes even more explicit and intense:

- When we are training others, we are more consciously trying to change them—especially in ways related to performance outcomes.

- When we are training, we have been given explicit permission to try to change others, either by the participants or their bosses or both.

- When we are training others, we are presenting ourselves as experts—more than normally able to change others in the ways they wish to be changed.

As trainers, then, what differentiates our workshop environments from everyday communication is simply that we have special opportunity and power to influence and that we are held especially responsible for what we communicate. Therefore, we contend, we have a special responsibility to be clear about our desired outcomes.

So, let's look at the categories previously illustrated:

When we design training we are attempting to affect others' knowledge, skills, or attitudes.

Knowledge = information.

Skills = an ability to do something.

Attitude = a mind-set or feeling about something.

When you are designing a session, are you always clear which of those you are aiming to affect? Do the activities you choose align with your learning objectives? Interactive activities are great; fun is fun; but if you are not clear on what the POINT of your story or activity is—in what way you are trying to change a participant—you are squandering that special influence you have been granted.

Improv games can address all three areas. Often, one activity can be applied in a variety of ways that target different objectives. Here is a way to think about activities and link them to knowledge, skills, and attitudes:

*Jolts* are activities that affect people's attitudes and beliefs. They produce "aha" moments. Usually they work once.

*Exercises* are activities that build skills and provide practice. They can be played over and over again without losing their impact, like machines at the gym.

*Frame games* are templates or shells into which any content can be placed. They are useful for imparting knowledge and assessing retention and understanding. When using improv games in this way, the principles of improv become less important. The game simply provides an opportunity to engage the learners in an active way.

Again, many activities can fit into more than one of the design categories. The point is to know the point. In this context, let me offer an exercise (which may also serve as a jolt).

Think about something you teach. Figure out whether you want to use an activity to address a knowledge, skill, or attitude gap in the learner. Choose an activity that is the aligned jolt, exercise, or frame game to best meet that need. Repeat as needed.

## Facilitating Improv Activities

With the help of countless colleagues, and in response to a specific request at the Applied Improvisation Network Conference in Baltimore, 2011, the following Top-10 List for facilitating improv activities in the workplace was created. I am delighted to share it with you here. Many of these tips can be found in the previous chapters, but for expediency, here is the list in its streamlined form:

1. Know your objective. Improv is no different from any other learning and development intervention. You must know what you are trying to accomplish. Ask yourself "What do I want the participants to DO differently when they leave here?"

2. Focus on your partner. The workshop participants are your partners. It is all about them. Keith Johnstone often criticized the emcees in his format, Theatresports, for competing for the limelight instead of simply holding the space and providing a context for the performers to perform. Anything you do—including being charismatic or funny—should support your objective and add value for the learners, not just make you feel smart or attractive or important.

3. Acknowledge and celebrate failure. Things don't always go according to plan, or well for that matter. As we are encouraging our learners to take risks and try on new performances, we must also be willing to try new things, adapt to the needs and styles of the learners in the room, and acknowledge and celebrate when activities don't work. San Francisco–based improviser and trainer, Diane Rachel, gives a great example of

saying, "Well, that didn't go the way I planned! Whoo hoo!" People notice and are delighted when you demonstrate that you, too, are fallible and willing to grow.

4. Safe is different from comfortable. This is one of my personal favorites and one that I credit my colleagues at Performance of a Lifetime with bringing home to me. I used to believe that creating a safe environment meant not requiring anyone to do anything that made them uncomfortable. Then it became clear that "comfortable" was the wrong goal. In some ways it is the opposite of the goal. Learning and growing are by definition about moving outside our "comfort zones." Creating safety means creating an environment (and a mind-set) in which one can seek out, and sit with, discomfort in order to stretch and grow. Just like working out at the gym or doing yoga. Ask yourself: What can I do to support the participants in trying NEW performances and gathering NEW insights.

5. "Yes, and" the participants. Or as our guru, Thiagi, would say, "Let the inmates run the asylum." If you don't really want to know about participants' experience of an activity or their answers to your questions, don't ask! If you do ask, honor their input—even if it is not what you were expecting, or like, or wanted. If we are really good we should be hugely prepared, and completely willing to throw away our plan if it turns out our agenda is not aligned with the needs of the learners.

6. Dare to be dull. As I was about to run a foundational and familiar game as an example of a nonverbal leadership exercise, to an audience of applied improv facilitators, I thought, *Geez, everyone here is going to know this game. What do I have that's clever and original and impressive?* As teachers, many of us like new things and want to feel exciting and clever and original and innovative. But the good old staples are staples because they are great. They are simple and clear and foundational. And for many of your participants your old activities are fresh, even revelatory. My father used to talk about how orchestras like to play obscure modern pieces, but audiences want to hear Beethoven's 9th. Use the game that meets your objective best, not the one that is most exciting to

you. (See Tips 1, 2, and 5.) Of course, new games can be good, too. The times to try new games are when you feel you need something that meets a specific need better than the material you have. Or when you need to do something fresh to keep yourself focused and developing.

7. Show, don't tell. Experiential learning is valuable because it is experiential. Do not tell the participants—before or after the game—what their experience will or should be. Ask, listen, respect, and build from their comments.

8. Debrief. "An activity is just an excuse for a good debrief," says the incomparable Thiagi. Tip 7 notwithstanding, we do not learn from our experience, we learn from examining our experience. Think about your objective and structure your debriefing in service of it. Here are Thiagi's famous and fabulous Six Phases of Debriefing questions useful for any activity in any circumstance:

   • How do you feel?

   • What happened?

   • What did you learn?

   • How does this relate to the real world?

   • What if? (e.g., What if we played with strangers; What if I told you you were wrong after every offer? . . .)

   • What next? (Thiagi Newsletter, February 2004, www .thiagi.com/pfp/IE4H/february2004.html)

9. Respect differences. Use activities that are varied. Respect different behavioral and learning styles. Even within improv, there are activities that appeal to introverts and extroverts, the verbal and nonverbal, those who like to think outside and inside the box. Do not just choose your favorites. Mix it up.

10. Trust yourself. Improv is valuable. It is not just a metaphor. We are all improvising all the time. Do not oversell. Trust that if you thought about Tips 1 and 2, your participants WILL see value.

If investment bankers and physicians and steel company executives can play these games, so can your learners.

One final note, please feel free to adapt these exercise and use them for purposes other than those specified here. After all, that kind of innovation is what improv is all about. And when you do, we would love to hear about how it goes. Happy playing!

# Accept This!

*Overview:*
- In pairs, participants take turns making neutral, innocuous statements and over-accepting them. (See chapter 4—Accepting Offers.)

*Improv Topic:*
- Accepting offers
- Spontaneity

*Purpose:*
- Warm-up
- Energy builder
- Team building
- Creativity
- Communication

*Supplies:*
- None

*Time:*
- 8–15 minutes

*Number of Players:*
- Pairs

*Game Flow:*
- Have the participants get into pairs.
- Pick an A and a B.
- Have the As make some kind of neutral statement (e.g., "It's sunny today." "The report is due on the 17th." "You are wearing black shoes.").
- Have the Bs respond to the offer with a huge emotion and rant about the ramifications of the statement. For example, "I'm wearing black

shoes? Oh, no! I thought they were brown. Now my shoes and my pants won't match. My mother is coming to visit today, and when she sees that my shoes and pants don't match, she will humiliate me in front of everyone. I will probably lose my job and eventually be homeless. . . ." (See page 53 for further examples and discussion.)
- When B finishes, have her make a neutral statement to A, who responds with a different huge emotion and begins a rant.
  The two participants switch back and forth as often as time allows.

*Variations:*
- Have the second person build off of a statement in the first person's rant.
- Provide the neutral statements on slips of paper.
- Provide the emotion with which participants respond.
- Have participants play in groups of four, with the participants responding to each statement in pairs.
- Play in a circle, with participants taking turns directing a statement to someone across the circle, who responds.
- Give the participants a process or product and have them rant about the value of it or how it has impacted their lives. (This version is a good review activity or idea-generation exercise.)

*Tips:*
- Encourage the participants to have huge, outrageous responses. They need not be logical.
- Encourage the participants to choose different emotions each time they respond.
- The versions in which participants are playing in pairs at the same time will be less stressful for the participants.
- You may wish to model the activity to increase the participants' willingness to take risks.

*Suggested Debrief Questions:*
- What happens when you over-accept?
- How did it feel to express yourself with emotion?
- What emotions were easiest for you to express?

- How did you censor yourself?
- What is the value of accepting and building on offers?
- What does this activity have to do with creativity?

*Source:*
- Adapted from Keith Johnstone's "It's Tuesday" exercise.

# Ask a Silly Question

*Overview:*
- Quickly fire off silly questions and call on participants to answer them as spontaneously as they can. For example, "What does an elephant wear to bed?" "How do people cook spaghetti on Mars?" "Why does a bear snore?" There are no wrong answers, save not saying something.

*Improv Topic:*
- Spontaneity
- Accepting offers
- Trust

*Purpose:*
- Icebreaker
- Warm-up
- Energy builder
- Team building
- Creativity

*Supplies:*
- None

*Time:*
- 3–8 minutes

*Number of Players:*
- Various

*Game Flow:*
- Tell the participants that you are going to quiz them.
- The good news is that anything they say is right.
- Ask silly questions and encourage the respondents to answer as quickly as possible, saying whatever comes to mind. Some sample questions are:
  - How do you turn bubblegum into gold?
  - Why do monkeys play the cymbals?
  - Why is the moon made of cheese?
  - What are the three friendliest colors?
  - What do you mush in a mushroom?

*Variations:*
- Have participants play in pairs, or groups of three or four, taking turns asking and answering questions.
- Play in a circle with each person giving a question to the person on their right.
- Hand out a written sheet of questions and have a competition for the participant who can finish first. Then have everyone share their answers.

*Tips:*
- Coach participants to answer quickly and say anything.
- Ask open-ended questions, rather than ones that elicit "yes" or "no" answers.
- The sillier the question, the better. Participants will be more willing to be spontaneous if it is very clear that there are no "right" answers.
- As the facilitator, you may want to create some silly questions ahead of time. It may be significantly harder to come up with silly questions than to answer them.

*Suggested Debrief Questions:*
- What happened when I told you there would be a quiz?
- How did you feel when I said any answer was right?
- How did you censor yourself?
- What felt good?
- What is the value of saying the first thing that comes to mind?
- What is the value of asking silly questions?

*Source:*
- Adapted from Kenn Adams and Freestyle Repertory Theatre.

# Awareness Quiz

*Overview:*
- Participants begin by having short conversations in pairs. Then they stand with their backs to their partners with their eyes closed. The facilitator asks questions about the partners' appearance, which each person answers silently to themselves. Then the pairs turn to each other and check their observational accuracy.

*Improv Topic:*
- Listening and awareness

*Purpose:*
- Warm-up
- Energy builder
- Team building
- Creativity
- Communication

*Supplies:*
- None

*Time:*
- 3–5 minutes

*Number of Players:*
- Pairs

*Game Flow:*
- Have each participant find a partner.
- Ask them to introduce themselves or have a short conversation. (One possible topic is to find two or three things that they have in common that they did not already know about.)
- Have the pairs stand back-to-back with their eyes closed.
  Ask the following questions and have the participants answer silently to themselves:
  - What kind of shoes is your partner wearing? What color are they? How do they fasten? Can you see their socks? If so what do they look like? Are they wearing socks at all?

- What are they wearing on the bottom? Pants? A skirt? What color? Material? How does it fasten? Are they wearing a belt?
- What kind of shirt are they wearing? Color? Material? What's the neckline like? Are there buttons? What are the sleeves like?
- Are they wearing jewelry? What kind?
- What is their hair like? Color? Length? How is it styled?
- Are they wearing glasses? Do they have facial hair?
- What color are their eyes?
- Once you have asked all the questions, have the partners turn around and check their accuracy.

*Variations:*
- Ask the participants questions about the environment. How many windows? What color is the carpet? And so on.
- Ask the participants questions about their own watches.
- Practice individually by closing your eyes at various times and quizzing yourself on your observation of your desk phone, the bus you are on, your car dashboard and so on.
- Have the participants close their eyes for 60 seconds and note all the sounds that they hear.

*Tips:*
- When playing in pairs, you may wish to play the "Classic Mirror" exercise (page 148) before engaging in "Awareness Quiz."
- Coach the participants to remain silent during the exercise.
- Give the participants a few moments to check in with each other and chat before debriefing as an entire group.

*Suggested Debrief Questions:*
- How did you do? Anyone get 100%? Anyone get nothing?
- What kinds of things do we notice? Why?
- Why do we block out so much information?
- How do we decide what to pay attention to?
- How much better would you have done, had I asked you to study the other person ahead of time?

- What does this tell us about our powers of observation?
- How can we improve our levels of awareness?

*Source:*
- Adapted from Patricia Ryan, improv instructor, Stanford University, and David K. Reynolds, PhD.

# Ball Ball

*Overview:*
- The participants stand in a circle, tossing a soft volleyball around, attempting to keep it in the air for as long as possible. No one may tap the ball more than once in a row, and the ball may not touch the ground.

*Improv Topic:*
- Accepting offers
- Listening and awareness
- Trust

*Purpose:*
- Icebreaker
- Warm-up
- Energy builder
- Team building
- Communication
- Needs assessment
- Review
- Closing

*Supplies:*
- None

*Time:*
- 7–15 minutes

*Number of Players:*
- 4–20

*Game Flow:*
- Participants stand in a circle.
- One person tosses a ball into the air.
- Participants hit the ball to each other, keeping it from touching the ground for as long as possible. No one may hit the ball more than once in a row.
- Participants count the hits out loud as they go.

*Variations:*

- As a needs-assessment activity, have participants shout out issues they have or things they would like to get from the training, rather than numbers.
- As a review activity, have the participants shout out learning points from the training.
- As a brainstorming activity, have the participants shout out ideas.
- Have the participants tell a story one word at a time, shouting out the word as they hit the ball.
- Play with two or three balls.

*Tips:*

- This simple game highlights the main skills of teamwork. You may wish to talk about "hogging the ball," "wimping out," and the variety of skills that help the team accomplish even such a simple goal.
- Find a soft ball that will not hurt people's hands or heads. A ball the size of a soccer ball, but softer, is best.

*Suggested Debrief Questions:*

- What helped us be successful?
- What hindered our process?
- How much were you willing to participate? Why?
- How did you feel when the team dropped the ball?
- How did you feel when you thought you were responsible? When someone else was?
- How did individuals support each other?
- How is this like real life?

*Source:*

- Rebecca Stockley and Bay Area Theatresports, via Craig Turner, University of Washington, based on the work of Jacques LeCoq.

# Ball Toss

*Overview:*
- Participants throw a series of balls around in a set pattern, adding as many balls as they can. Eventually, the group can break out of the circle, and additional objectives may be added.

*Improv Topic:*
- Trust
- Accepting offers
- Listening and awareness

*Purpose:*
- Icebreaker
- Warm-up
- Energy builder
- Team building
- Communication
- Closing

*Supplies:*
- 5–10 soft juggling balls or sacks

*Time:*
- 10–30 minutes

*Number of Players:*
- 6–20

*Game Flow:*
- Have the participants stand in a circle.
- One person throws the ball to someone across the circle.
- That person puts her hand on her head to indicate that she has been thrown to and then throws the ball to someone else across the circle. This pattern continues until everyone has thrown and received the ball once.
- Then the pattern is repeated, with each participant continuing to throw and receive from the same person each time.
- As the team improves, the leader adds more and more balls.

- After the pattern is established and a number of balls are in play, ask the group members to walk randomly around the room, continuing to throw and receive from the same people.
- Finally, play different rounds, asking the participants to achieve different objectives. These objectives may include:
  - never drop a ball
  - throw the balls as quickly as possible
  - throw the ball as far as possible

*Variations:*
- Play passing various objects—a ball, a Frisbee, a beach ball, a chair (which should be passed, not thrown).
- Play with different objects being passed in different patterns.

*Tips:*
- Make sure the group remembers the original pattern before adding objects.
- Remind the group that the objective is to make the other people look good. Tell them that if their partner drops the ball, it is their responsibility. (See chapter 4—Accepting Offers—for further discussion.)
- Remind the group of the "no one gets hurt" rule. Use soft objects or require that a heavier object (like a chair) is passed, not thrown.
- As a final round, you may ask the participants to choose a private, individual objective and see what happens.

*Suggested Debrief Questions:*
- What helped us achieve our task?
- What stood in the way?
- What happened when I suggested that it was your responsibility to ensure that you partner caught the ball?
- What effect did changing the specific objectives have?
- How is this like real-life teamwork?

*Source:*
- Rebecca Stockley.

# Blindfold Walk

*Overview:*
- In pairs, have the participants take turns leading and following. The follower closes her eyes, and the leader guides her around the space without touching her, by calling her name.

*Improv Topic:*
- Trust
- Listening and awareness
- Nonverbal behavior

*Purpose:*
- Warm-up
- Team building
- Communication

*Supplies:*
- None

*Time:*
- 10–20 minutes

*Number of Players:*
- Pairs

*Game Flow:*
- Demo this activity with a volunteer before engaging the entire group.
- Divide the participants into pairs.
- Have each pair choose an A and a B.
- Have the As close their eyes and the Bs lead them around the space by calling their name.
- Instruct the participants that the most important rule is that no one gets hurt, so they may say "stop" or touch their partners, if it looks like their safety is at risk. Otherwise they should refrain from saying anything but their partners' names.
- After a few minutes, have the As and Bs switch roles.

*Variations:*
- Have the leaders hold the hands of the followers, rather than call their names.

- Have the leaders use language.
- Have one leader with her eyes open and two to four followers holding hands behind with their eyes closed.

*Tips:*
- Emphasize the safety and trust aspects of the game. Monitor the participants as they go.
- The more room there is to explore, the more interesting the game is. Allow participants to go outside the workshop room, if possible— through doorways, along halls, up and down stairs.

*Suggested Debrief Questions:*
- How did it feel to follow?
- How did it feel to lead?
- Which role were you most comfortable in?
- What did you explore?
- How many risks did you take?
- Did trust increase or decrease? Why?

*Source:*
- Adapted from Viola Spolin.

# But Versus And

*Overview:*
- Two groups set about the task of planning a company party. The first must start each sentence with the words, "*Yes, but.*" The second must start their sentences with the words, "*Yes, and.*" The first group will struggle to achieve anything. The second will create much more easily. (See page 46.)

*Improv Topic:*
- Accepting offers
- Listening and awareness

*Purpose:*
- Team building
- Creativity
- Communication

*Supplies:*
- None

*Time:*
- 4–8 minutes

*Number of Players:*
- Various

*Game Flow:*
*Round 1*
- Ask for 3–5 volunteers.
- Tell the group that they are in charge of planning the company holiday party.
- Each person must contribute an idea. There is no specific order, but no one may contribute more than one idea in a row.
- Anyone may start, and each successive idea must begin with the words, "*Yes, but. . . .*"
- Allow the exercise to continue for 2–3 minutes, or until it degenerates beyond repair.

*Round 2*
- Ask for 3–5 new volunteers.

- Set up the same activity with the following adjustment: This time each new sentence must start with the words, *"Yes, and. . . ."*
- Allow the activity to continue for 2–3 minutes, or until the group seems satisfied and delighted.

*Variations:*
- Play simultaneously in pairs or groups up to five people. Allow each group to try both the "yes, but . . ." and the "yes, and . . ." versions.
- Assign a different task (e.g., create a meeting agenda; design a new product).
- Have the same group of five people demo both rounds.
- Role-play with some people saying "yes, and . . ." and some saying "yes, but. . . ."

*Tips:*
- Continue to remind participants to use the words *"Yes, and . . ."* or *"Yes, but. . . ."*
- End the rounds when the ideas trail off (usually in the first round) or on an explosion of approval (usually the second round).
- Pay attention to the intention of the statements. If the demonstration does not work, it may be because the participants are actually blocking, even though they are saying "yes, and . . ." or vice versa.

*Suggested Debrief Questions:*
- How does it feel to have your ideas rejected? Accepted?
- How did this experience compare to real life?
- Why do we block other people's ideas?
- How can we increase our willingness and ability to accept ideas?

*Source:*
- Viola Spolin, Keith Johnstone, Fratelli Bologna, Theatresports.

# Character Creation

*Overview:*
- As a group, the participants create a character, one feature or personality trait at a time. Beginning with a name, participants randomly take turns making offers until the character feels complete or the group loses a clear image of it.

*Improv Topic:*
- Spontaneity
- Listening and awareness
- Accepting offers
- Trust
- Storytelling
- Nonverbal behavior

*Purpose:*
- Warm-up
- Team building
- Creativity
- Communication

*Supplies:*
- None

*Time:*
- 10–20 minutes

*Number of Players:*
- 2–20

*Game Flow:*
- Have the participants sit in a circle.
- Provide (or ask the group for) a fictional first and last name of a character (e.g., Sally McMurphy, Renaldo Hernandez, Clyde Clump, Isadora Ilandavalle).
- Have the participants randomly offer characteristics, building on the offers of others (e.g., "Sally McMurphy is a waitress." "She has huge green eyes." "She came to America from Ireland two years ago." "She came because her family was really poor, and she wanted to seek her fortune.").

- If someone in the group loses the picture of the character, because he feels an offer contradicts something that has already been said or just doesn't make sense, he can say, "I can't see it," and the group will begin again with a new character.
- End work on a character when the group can no longer see it or feels the description is complete.
- Play as many rounds as you wish.

*Variations:*
- Have the group describe an environment (e.g., a hotel room, a haunted house, a train station, an office, a barn).
- Have the group describe a fictional product (e.g., Wiggy Wash, Yum-yum Paste, Ever-clean, Box-in-a-box).
- Have the group describe a character beginning with a characteristic other than a name (e.g., a profession, an age, a nationality, a physical characteristic).
- Have the group describe the future state of the team (see "Vision Weaving," page 227).

*Tips:*
- Encourage the group to speak up when they lose the vision of the character in the beginning. This allows the group to assess the kinds of risks they are willing to take and take a look at their assumptions.
- For use as an exercise on accepting offers, as the exercise progresses, encourage the participants to expand their ability to "see" characteristics that they were rejecting at first.
- Encourage the group to take their time.
- If a few members are dominating, ask for input from those who have not yet offered suggestions.
- This exercise can be used in diversity training to explore stereotypes. What characteristics do we associate with others? What are we unwilling to "see"?

*Suggested Debrief Questions:*
- How did we work together? How aligned did you feel with the group vision?
- How did it feel to have your ideas accepted? Rejected?

- How did you censor yourself?
- What does this tell us about creating collaboratively?
- How do you feel about the people we created?
- What characteristics did we associate with others?
- Which characteristics did we see as incompatible?
- How does this translate to real interpersonal interactions?

*Source:*
- Adapted from Keith Johnstone.

# Circle Mirror

*Overview:*
- Everyone stands in a circle and identifies someone across the circle to watch, so that each person is looking at a different member of the group. Then members of the group begin in neutral positions and "mirror" or copy each other's movements and facial expressions. No one attempts to initiate any movement.

*Improv Topic:*
- Trust
- Listening and awareness
- Nonverbal behavior

*Purpose:*
- Energy builder
- Team building
- Creativity
- Communication

*Supplies:*
- None

*Time:*
- 5–7 minutes

*Number of Players:*
- 6–20

*Game Flow:*
- Have the participants form a circle.
- One by one, have individuals choose someone across the circle to watch. This can be done by having the first person point to someone and then put their hand on their head to show they have been taken. The person pointed to does the same thing until everyone has pointed and been pointed to once.
- Check the pattern by having everyone point to the person they are watching.
- Ask everyone to stand in a neutral position—feet shoulder width apart; arms down at their sides; head straight.

- Tell the group that they are not to initiate any movement intentionally, but that they should vigilantly mirror the person that they have chosen to watch.
- Start the game.

*Variations:*
- Play sitting in chairs.
- Play a more traditional mirror activity in which one person leads and everyone else follows.
- Begin with the traditional form and then, after a few moments, instruct the participants to initiate and follow collaboratively, without having any leader specified.

*Tips:*
- The results of this exercise will be that the group will start moving more and more—big gestures, facial expressions and movements, without anyone consciously initiating. This illustrates how many offers we make that we are unaware of.
- Double-check the pattern. If any of the links of people watching is broken, the exercise will not work.

*Suggested Debrief Questions:*
- What happened?
- Did anyone consciously initiate?
- Who assumed that someone had to be cheating?
- What does this mean?
- If we are making more offers than we are aware of, what are the ramifications?
- What does this tell us about communication?

*Source:*
- Adapted from Viola Spolin, Ruth Zapora, East Bay improv instructor, Patricia Ryan, and Rebecca Stockley.

# Classic Mirror

*Overview:*
- In pairs, participants "mirror" each other—moving at the same time as if one were the other's reflection. The two take turns leading and following and then finally attempt to move together, with both leading and following at the same time.

*Improv Topic:*
- Listening and awareness
- Trust
- Nonverbal behavior

*Purpose:*
- Warm-up
- Team building
- Communication

*Supplies:*
- None

*Time:*
- 8–15 minutes

*Number of Players:*
- Pairs

*Game Flow:*
- Have the participants form pairs.
- Have the pairs face each other and pick an A and a B.
- Assign Bs to be the leaders and As to be the followers. Explain that any movement that the leader makes, the follower will copy, as if they are a mirror image. (If the leader moves her right hand, the follower will move his left as he faces her.)
- After a few minutes of Bs leading, instruct the pairs to switch leaders.
- After a few minutes of As leading, instruct the pairs to pass the lead back and forth at their own discretion until they themselves are unsure who is leading and who is following.
- Debrief.

*Variations:*
- Assign the pairs a specific activity (e.g., brushing their teeth).
- Play music in the background.
- Play as a group in a circle. (See "Circle Mirror," page 146.)

*Tips:*
- Ask the participants to play silently.
- Coach the participants to take care of their partners—if the follower can't keep up, it is the leader's responsibility to slow down.
- Remind the followers that they are responding as if they are a mirror reflection. Coach them individually, if need be.

*Suggested Debrief Questions:*
- Were you more comfortable leading or following?
- What happened as the exercise progressed?
- What kind of risks did you take?
- How did you limit yourself?
- How did it feel to communicate without words?
- What are the characteristics of a good leader?
- What are the characteristics of a good follower?

*Source:*
- Adapted from Viola Spolin.

# Color/Advance

*Overview:*
- An activity to help flesh out the details of a story, and balance description with action.

*Improv Topic:*
- Storytelling
- Accepting offers
- Listening and awareness
- Spontaneity

*Purpose:*
- Creativity
- Communication
- Needs assessment
- Problem solving
- Review

*Supplies:*
- A flip chart, slide, or handout with the Story Spine recorded.

*Time:*
- 5–15 minutes

*Number of Players:*
- Pairs

*Game Flow:*
- Divide participants into pairs.
- Ask each pair to choose a storyteller and a guide.
- The storyteller begins to tell a story.
- Periodically the guide pauses the storyteller and says, "Color the _____," instructing the storyteller to enhance some detail. ("Color" includes any kind of description—physical details, mood, inner thoughts and feelings—of the characters.)
- When the guide is satisfied, she coaches, "Advance," and the story-teller continues with the action of the story. ("Action" consists of anything that answers the question "What comes next?")

- Continue until the story is finished or time is up.
- Switch roles.
  (Note: Some trainers may wish to demonstrate this activity with a volunteer before having the pairs begin. If so, it is best for the facilitator to take the role of guide.)

*Variations:*
- Divide the participants into groups of three with two guides—one in charge of calling for color, one in charge of advancing.
- Have the participants write their stories individually, arbitrarily calling out "color" and "advance" from the front of the room.
- "Conducted Color/Advance"—Ask for three volunteers to tell a story. Assign one to be in charge of action, one in charge of physical description, and one in charge of inner emotions and thoughts. Conduct the story by pointing to each person and have him or her continue the story focusing on his or her task. (See "Conducted Narrative," page 153.)
- Teach workshop participants the "Color/Advance" vocabulary and allow them to color and advance your lectures.

*Tips:*
- Coach the guides to limit their input to saying, "color" or "advance." They should not ask questions (e.g., "What's inside the box?") or offer suggestions (e.g., "He marries the waitress, right?").
- Let the guides know that they can coach "color" or "advance" for two reasons: to help the story and to "work" the storyteller.
- Remind the storyteller that part of the value of the exercise is to be able to distinguish between description and action, and that they should commit to doing one or the other, without moving on until they are coached to.

*Suggested Debrief Questions:*
- Coaches, how did you decide when to call "color" and "advance"?
- Storytellers, how did it feel to be led?
- Was one activity easier than the other?
- What sorts of items did you color?
- How did the action and the description feed each other?

- How compelling were the stories that your partners told?
- How many of you feel like you are better storytellers than you thought?

*Source:*
- Adapted from Viola Spolin and Freestyle Repertory Theatre.

# Conducted Narrative

*Overview:*
- Four or five participants tell a story together, each person speaking when they are pointed to by a "conductor." Whenever the next person is pointed to, she must continue exactly where her partner left off—in the middle of a sentence or word.

*Improv Topic:*
- Storytelling
- Listening and awareness
- Accepting offers
- Spontaneity

*Purpose:*
- Warm-up
- Team building
- Creativity
- Communication
- Review

*Supplies:*
- None

*Time:*
- 3–6 minutes per round

*Number of Players:*
- 4–5 per round

*Game Flow:*
- Ask for four or five volunteers.
- Tell the participants that they will tell a story.
- Explain that the person that you point to will talk. When you point to someone else, that person will continue wherever the previous person left off, even if it is in the middle of a sentence or word.
- Get a suggested title for a never-before-told story from the observers and begin.
- Continue until the story is finished.

*Variations:*
- Assign two participants to be in charge of the action or plot and two to be in charge of the description. Each participant must only describe or advance the action, based on their job.
- Play as an elimination game (see "Elimination Lists," page 160) in which participants who make mistakes are eliminated and another participant from the large group takes their place. In this case, mistakes include: pausing too long before speaking, saying something that does not follow cleanly from the phrase or word before, or echoing (repeating) the last word that was said.
- Play simultaneously in subgroups of four or five, with participants taking turns conducting each other.
- As a review activity, give the participants a process or concept to describe.
- Provide a genre or style of story. This version is good for inspiring people to think in different ways. It is also beneficial for exploring storytelling structures.

*Tips:*
- When conducting, make eye contact with the speakers and point with big, clear gestures.
- If the story gets completely muddled, begin a new one.
- Encourage the participants to be obvious and simple. With four people telling a story, there will be plenty of strangeness anyway.
- Have the participants tell the stories in the third person/past tense. That will allow action to take place and a consistent character voice to be maintained.
- See chapter 6, Storytelling, for more general tips on storytelling skills.

*Suggested Debrief Questions:*
- What did you think of our stories?
- What was difficult? What was easy?
- How did you censor yourself?
- What made the story compelling?
- How was this different from telling a story yourself?
- What is the value of creating collaboratively?

- What are the pitfalls or frustrations?
- How does this relate to teamwork on the job?

*Source:*
- Adapted from Del Close's "Conducted Story," Chicago City Limits and Theatresports.

# Conversation Weave

*Overview:*
- Three or four participants tell stories as if they are talking to a friend. The individuals speak a few sentences at a time and then let someone else speak. The stories are unrelated, but the participants weave details and words from the other stories into their own.

*Improv Topic:*
- Listening and awareness
- Accepting offers
- Storytelling

*Purpose:*
- Team building
- Creativity
- Communication

*Supplies:*
- None

*Time:*
- 8–15 minutes per group

*Number of Players:*
- 3 or 4 per group

*Game Flow:*
- Three or four volunteers stand in front of the group.
- Assign a topic or theme.
- One of the participants starts to tell a story. After a few sentences, he stops, and a second participant starts her story. Then the next person starts.
- After the stories have been established, the individuals take turns randomly offering new parts of their stories a few sentences at a time.
- As they continue with their stories, the participants weave words from the other stories into their own.

*Variations:*
- Conduct the participant by pointing to them, or calling out the name of the next person to speak.

- Have the participants act as if they are speaking on the phone, and have them weave the other conversations into theirs.
- Have three pairs of participants role-play conversations and weave in words from the other conversations.

*Tips:*
- Encourage the participants to weave in the words without letting their stories become the same.
- Coach (or conduct) the participants to increase the speed with which they switch speakers as the exercise advances.

*Suggested Debrief Questions:*
- Observers, what did you notice? What was compelling about this activity?
- Storytellers, which words or phrases stood out to you?
- Did this activity make the storytelling easier or more difficult?
- How does this activity relate to real life?
- How can we use this ability to increase creativity and communication?

*Source:*
- Adapted from Del Close's "Cocktail Party," and Chicago Improv School's "Telephone Bank."

# Declare Yourself

*Overview:*
- The participants stand in a circle. One by one, they step forward into the center of the circle, make eye contact with the other members, and say, "I am (*name*), and I am here."

*Improv Topic:*
- Trust
- Listening and awareness
- Nonverbal behavior

*Purpose:*
- Icebreaker
- Warm-up
- Team building
- Communication
- Needs assessment
- Review
- Closing

*Supplies:*
- None

*Time:*
- 5–15 minutes

*Number of Players:*
- 3–20

*Game Flow:*
- Have the participants stand in a circle.
- One at a time, as they feel the impulse to, each participant takes a step toward the center of the circle.
- First the person who has stepped forward looks around the circle, making eye contact with the other participants.
- Then he says, "I am (*name*), and I am here."
- After a moment, he steps back, and someone else steps forward.

*Variations:*
- Have the participants state their intention for a meeting or workshop (e.g., I intend to improve my ability to give effective feedback). This is an effective needs assessment activity.
- Have the participants step forward and make eye contact with everyone in silence.
- End a workshop by having participants share one thing that they learned in the session.

*Tips:*
- Encourage the participants to take their time.
- There should be no talking other than the words of the person stepping forward.
- In its pure form, this activity is surprisingly powerful. Make sure to create a safe space for potential vulnerability.

*Suggested Debrief Questions:*
- How did this feel?
- What surprised you?
- What was the most difficult part?
- What does this tell you about giving a presentation? About communication in general?
- How do you feel as a team now?

*Source:*
- Adapted from Patricia Ryan's "I Am Here."

# Elimination Lists

*Overview:*
- Four or five participants stand in front of the group. The facilitator assigns a category (or gets one from the group) and points to individual participants. Each participant must name something that fits into that category (e.g., Category: Breakfast cereals. Participants: "Cheerios," "Fruit Loops," "Oatmeal"). If a participant makes a mistake, they are eliminated, and another person takes their place.

*Improv Topic:*
- Spontaneity
- Listening and awareness
- Trust

*Purpose:*
- Icebreaker
- Warm-up
- Energy builder
- Team building
- Creativity
- Communication
- Review

*Supplies:*
- None

*Time:*
- 6–12 minutes

*Number of Players:*
- 4–20 (or more with increased time, or if some behave as observers only)

*Game Flow:*
- Ask for four or five volunteers.
- Instruct them that you will get a category from the observers. When you point to each participant, you want them to name something that fits into that category.
- If they make a mistake, it is the job of the observers to make a buzzer sound, "aaaaaaannnhhhhh," and the one who made the mistake will be eliminated.

- Explain that a mistake consists of one of three things: pausing too long before saying something, saying something that has already been said, or saying something that does not fit into the category.
- Ask the remaining participants for a category and begin.
- Each time someone is eliminated, get a new volunteer to take their place and a new category.
- Continue the activity, ideally, until all participants have had the chance to play.

*Variations:*
- As a review activity, assign the topic yourself.
- Play with the entire group at the same time, eliminating people until you have one grand prize winner.
- Have participants take turns conducting the activity.

*Tips:*
- This activity is useful for discussing the value of failing gracefully.
- Encourage the participants to take a big bow when they make a mistake.
- Increase the speed as the activity continues.
- Use clear, big gestures and make eye contact with the participants while conducting.

*Suggested Debrief Questions:*
- Why was that fun?
- How did you feel when you made a mistake?
- How did you feel when someone else made a mistake?
- What helped you do well at this activity?
- Why is it so hard to think of something to say, when there are so many choices?
- How would we get better at this?
- What happened as the activity continued? Did you want to play more or less?
- What does this have to do with creativity and teamwork?

*Source:*
- Adapted from Del Close's "Conducted Story" and Theatresports.

# Emotional Meeting

*Overview:*

- Four people role-play having a meeting. They enter the room one at a time with a different emotional attitude. Each time a new person enters the room, everyone takes on their emotion. When the individuals leave, in reverse order, the remaining group reverts to the previous emotion.

*Improv Topic:*

- Trust
- Spontaneity
- Accepting offers
- Listening and awareness
- Nonverbal behavior

*Purpose:*

- Energy builder
- Team building
- Communication

*Supplies:*

- Chairs and table (optional)
- Flip chart and markers (optional)

*Time:*

- 5–10 minutes per group

*Number of Players:*

- 3–5 per group

*Game Flow:*

- Ask for three to five volunteers.
- Tell them that they are going to role-play a meeting. One by one, they will enter and then leave over the course of about 5 minutes.
- Assign each individual an emotion or attitude. (You can field them from the rest of the group. Get a variety. For example: joy, anger, fear, ambition.)
- Assign an order for the individuals to enter the playing area and review all the emotions.

- Let the group know that whenever a new person enters, they are all to take on that emotion.
- Then, explain that after the last person has been in the room for a while, she will leave and everyone will revert to the previous emotion, until the next person leaves, and so on, until the last person is left with his original emotion.
- Run the activity.

*Variations:*
- Play "Emotional Carpool" in which the members are in a car and pick up individuals on their way to work and then drop them off.
- Play in gibberish.
- Play silently.

*Tips:*
- Gather disparate emotions for each round.
- Be prepared to coach from the side as the activity progresses. Remind people what the current emotion is, if they forget, and prompt people to enter or leave.
- Expect raucous fun.

*Suggested Debrief Questions:*
- Why was this fun?
- How does this experience mirror real meetings?
- What effect does taking on others' feelings have?
- How can we use this effect for good?
- Can we control our emotions? How? Do we want to? Why?
- Which emotions served the meeting best?

*Source:*
- Adapted from the Chicago schools, Freestyle Repertory Theatre, Theatresports.

# Expert Interviews

*Overview:*
- One participant role-plays a subject-matter expert, and another plays an interviewer. The rest of the participants act as a studio audience, observing and asking questions.

*Improv Topic:*
- Spontaneity
- Accepting offers
- Listening and awareness
- Trust
- Storytelling
- Nonverbal behavior

*Purpose:*
- Team building
- Creativity
- Communication
- Needs assessment
- Problem solving
- Review

*Supplies:*
- Two chairs

*Time:*
- 7–15 minutes per group

*Number of Players:*
- Pairs

*Game Flow:*
- Ask for two volunteers, one to be the expert, one the interviewer.
- Assign an area of expertise to the expert. (This can be chosen by the facilitator or fielded from the participants.)
- Remind the two players to "yes, and . . ." each other.
- Have the interviewer introduce the guest and interview her.
- After a bit, have the audience ask questions.
- Debrief.

*Variations:*
- Have two or three experts with different attitudes or approaches to the topic.
- Have an expert made up of three participants who answer the questions one word at a time. (See "One-Word-at-a-Time Exercises," page 186)
- Have an expert who speaks gibberish and an interpreter who translates for him and the interviewer who speaks English. (See "Gibberish Press Conference," page 166).

*Tips:*
- For general creativity or communication skills training, pick an outrageous topic (e.g., fish playing basketball) or a topic that no one in the room knows much about. This diminishes the pressure to get the answers "right."
- For visioning and problem solving, use topics that participants are real experts in and use the format to focus their thinking and tap ideas they may not have thought of.
- Coach the expert to answer "yes" to the questions.
- Coach the interviewers to build on the previous answers when asking questions.

*Suggested Debrief Questions:*
- What happened when you said "yes" versus "no"?
- What surprised you?
- How did you censor yourself?
- When was this easiest?
- Why was this entertaining?

*Source:*
- Viola Spolin, the Chicago schools, and Theatresports.

# Gibberish Press Conference

*Overview:*
- One player speaks in a nonsense language, as if they were a foreign leader at a press conference. Another player translates the "gibberish" into English.

*Improv Topic:*
- Spontaneity
- Accepting offers
- Storytelling
- Nonverbal behavior

*Purpose:*
- Energy builder
- Team building
- Creativity
- Communication
- Review

*Supplies:*
- None

*Time:*
- 5–30 minutes

*Number of Players:*
- Pairs

*Game Flow:*
- Explain the concept of gibberish and demonstrate it.
- Have participants turn to a partner and say something in gibberish.
- Ask for two volunteers.
- Give the two a topic or have the other workshop participants provide one.
- Have one of the players speak in gibberish and the other translate.
- Allow the other participants to ask questions, which can be translated into gibberish by the interpreter.

*Variations:*
- Set up a talk show with a foreign guest, an interpreter, and a host who speaks English. The interpreter translates both the gibberish and the English.

- For presentation skills training, have participants practice their presentations completely in gibberish.
- Play gibberish poet, in which the interpreter translates a poem.
- Have a participant who speaks a foreign language that the group is not familiar with use their native tongue, rather than gibberish.
- In a circle, have the participants take turns translating a line of gibberish and then adding a line of their own, which is translated by the next person. This can be done as a continuous story or as unrelated phrases. (This activity can also be used as a warm-up activity for the other versions.)
- Dictate a story in gibberish, one line at a time. Have the participants write down their translations of your sentences as you go. Ask individuals to share their translations at the end.

*Tips:*
- Be gentle. When people are asked to make up nonsense, they can feel silly. Do not underestimate the risk you are asking certain individuals to take.
- Gibberish can be anything. If participants are resistant, coach them to say, "blah, blah, blah."
- Be willing to demonstrate gibberish to encourage others.
- Remind participants that whatever they say in English or in gibberish is right.
- Coach participants to say "yes" when asked a question.

*Suggested Debrief Questions:*
- How did it feel to communicate without words?
- What communication cues do we have other than words?
- Observers, did the translation match the interpretations you made in your heads?
- How did it feel to accept offers?
- How did it feel to have your offers accepted?
- What happens when we say "yes" versus saying "no"?
- In what ways did you censor yourself? Translators? Gibberish speakers?

*Source:*
- Adapted from Viola Spolin, the Chicago improv community, Freestyle Repertory Theatre, and Theatresports.

# Giving Gifts

*Overview:*
- In pairs, participants exchange imaginary gifts. One person hands the other an imaginary object. That person says, "Oh, it's a _____. Thanks!" Then he gives another gift to his partner. The participants continue to give and receive gifts back and forth for the duration of the activity.

*Improv Topic:*
- Accepting offers
- Spontaneity
- Trust
- Nonverbal behavior

*Purpose:*
- Icebreaker
- Warm-up
- Team building
- Creativity
- Communication

*Supplies:*
- None

*Time:*
- 5–15 minutes

*Number of Players:*
- Pairs

*Game Flow:*
- Divide the participants into pairs.
- Have the participants choose a Person A and a Person B.
- A presents B with an imaginary gift.
- B accepts and identifies the gift, saying, "Oh, it's a _____. Thank you! I love it."
- Then B gives A a gift, and so on.

*Variations:*
- Play silently.
- Play in a circle.

*Tips:*
- Explain that participants may be very specific with their physical indications or more general. (For example, the giver may mime unclasping a necklace or reading a book and then hand the object over. Or she might just put out her hands and offer up some nondescript object.)
- Remind the participants to accept the offer enthusiastically. Part of the exercise is arbitrary positive acceptance.
- Remind the participants that it is the receiver who ultimately defines the gift. If the giver unclasps what she thinks is a necklace and hands it over, and the receiver says, "Oh, it's a boa constrictor!" then, the object becomes a snake.
- Encourage the participants to go fast.
- Play for long enough that the participants exhaust their initial thoughts and move on to spontaneous invention.

*Suggested Debrief Questions:*
- How did it feel to receive the gifts?
- What was your experience of having to identify the gift?
- How did it feel to give gifts?
- What happened when your gift was identified as something other than what you intended?
- Which felt more comfortable, giving or receiving?
- How did the exercise change as it continued?
- What was your experience of having to accept the gifts with enthusiasm?
- What does this activity relate to real life?

*Source:*
- Viola Spolin, Keith Johnstone, and Freestyle Repertory Theatre.

# Group Counting

*Overview:*                                    20 - 1
- The members of the group count from 1 to 20 without deciding which participant will say the next number. There is no established pattern of who speaks next or tacit, conscious communication about order. Anyone may say the next number. If two or more people say a number at the same time, however, the group begins again with 1.

*Improv Topic:*
- Listening and awareness
- Trust

*Purpose:*
- Team building
- Communication
- Closing

*Supplies:*                          *Time:*
- None                               - 3–10 minutes

*Number of Players:*
- 4–20

*Game Flow:*
- Have the participants stand in a circle. 20 - 1
- Explain that the group will count from 1 to 20, in order, all whole numbers, no tricks.
- Have them close their eyes or focus on the center of the circle. (You may wish to place an object in the center to facilitate focus.)
- Each person can say a number whenever they wish, with the exception that they cannot say two numbers in a row.
- There is no established pattern or secret communication (e.g., no eye contact, no skipping every other person around the circle).
- Finally, and most importantly, whenever two or more people start to say a number at the same time, the group begins again with 1.

*Variations:*
- Count to 10 or 15.
- Continue to count until a mistake is made.
- Recite the alphabet one letter at a time.
- Tell a word-at-a-time story beginning with "Once" "upon" "a" "time," in which you start at the beginning of a new story each time more than one person says a word. (Note: This is a very advanced exercise and should only be tried after a group has gotten very good at counting.)

*Tips:*
- This exercise is the best I know for highlighting the idea that good teamwork depends on some ephemeral quality that is hard to identify. If you run this exercise on an ongoing basis, a group will quickly improve—counting to 60, 80, 100.
- Remind the group that there is not some secret trick. Counting to 20 one person at a time would be easy if you planned who went next. What's the fun in that?
- The secret to success is also not speed. If they are having a hard time, remind the participants to breathe and take their time.
- If there is a group of 15, and you are counting to 20, on average each member will get to say one to two numbers. That means if someone says three numbers, someone else must say none in order for the group to succeed. Remind the members of this if they are struggling.
- You may wish to coach the participants to "say a number when it is your turn—whatever that means to you." This phrase highlights the instinctual nature of the activity.
- Allow the group to fail. If they feel frustrated, coach them to take a deep breath, shake it off, and try again. Remind them of the tip you feel will be most useful.
- This is a great way to end a session. You may wish to let the exercise speak for itself without extensive debriefing.

*Suggested Debrief Questions:*
- How did that feel?
- When did you choose to say a number?
- When did you choose to stay silent?

- How did people contribute to success?
- Why do you think we're getting better at this? (Ask this question after a number of sessions.)
- How is this like group processes at work?

*Source:*
- Bay Area Theatresports, adapted from a Zen meditation practice.

# Hum Circle

*Overview:*
- The participants stand in a circle and, with their eyes closed, make sound, creating harmonies and musical patterns.

*Improv Topic:*
- Spontaneity
- Accepting offers
- Listening and awareness
- Trust

*Purpose:*
- Warm-up
- Team building
- Communication
- Closing

*Supplies:*
- None

*Time:*
- 5–10 minutes

*Number of Players:*
- 4–16 people

*Game Flow:*
- Have the participants stand in a circle with their shoulders touching.
- Instruct them to close their eyes or focus on the center of the circle, if they are more comfortable with that.
- Have them begin to hum as they feel the impulse. Each participant should listen to the others and contribute in response.
- Continue until the group discovers a natural ending.

*Variations:*
- Give the group a theme around which to create (e.g., winter, productivity, teamwork).
- Have the participants make all sorts of sounds in addition to humming.

- Give the participants simple musical instruments, like triangles, drums, maracas.
- Have the participants sit in chairs, in groups of four, and make music by humming or playing instruments.

*Tips:*
- Encourage the participants to take their time.
- Encourage them to make offers in response to other sounds.
- This activity can be a nice way to end a session.

*Suggested Debrief Questions:*
- How spontaneous did you feel?
- What moments do you remember?
- What kind of stories did you make up in your head?
- What kinds of emotions were elicited?
- How does this experience inform our work as a team?

*Source:*
- General acting training.

# I Failed!

*Overview:*
- Participants practice feeling comfortable being silly and making mistakes by taking huge bows and proclaiming, "I failed!" or "I made a mistake!" or "I feel silly!" while the other participants cheer.

*Improv Topic:*
- Spontaneity
- Trust

*Purpose:*
- Icebreaker
- Warm-up
- Energy builder
- Team building
- Creativity
- Communication
- Problem solving

*Supplies:*
- None

*Time:*
- 2–5 minutes

*Number of Players:*
- 2–1,000

*Game Flow:*
- Have all the participants raise their hands above their heads, as a gymnast might after a routine.
- Ask them to all proclaim with relish and pride, "I failed!" "I made a mistake!" "I feel stupid!"
- Then have them turn to someone next to them and take the position and state one of the phrases. Each person's partner cheers for them and then reciprocates.
- Finally, have the participants walk around the room practicing celebrating failure and applauding each other.

*Variations:*
- Have each person take a turn around the circle.
- Have participants play in groups of four or five.

*Tips:*
- Explain that it is only by making friends with failure that we will be willing to risk enough to succeed.
- This game is about acknowledging our discomfort and embracing it, rather than fleeing from it.
- Highlight for the participants that the phrases are "I FEEL silly," "I FEEL stupid"—not "I AM stupid."

*Suggested Debrief Questions:*
- Significant debrief not recommended for this activity.

*Source:*
- Theatresports.

# Idea Circle

*Overview:*
- The participants stand in a circle. The group passes an object (a ball, a stick, a shoe) around the circle, while one of the participants names all the words he can that begin with a specific letter. When the object gets around the circle to him, he stops and gives a new letter to the next person.

*Improv Topic:*
- Spontaneity

*Purpose:*
- Warm-up
- Energy builder
- Creativity
- Review

*Supplies:*
- One object

*Time:*
- 20–30 seconds per participant, per round

*Number of Players:*
- 10–20

*Game Flow:*
- Have the participants stand in a circle.
- Give the first participant an object that the group can pass around the circle (a ball, a stuffed animal, a juggling pin).
- Ask her to give the object to the person on her left and a letter of the alphabet to the person on her right.
- The person on the right then begins to name words that begin with that letter, while the group passes the object around the circle.
- As soon as the object gets to the person who is speaking, he stops.
- Then, he offers a letter to the person on his right and passes the object to the left. This continues until everyone has had a chance.

*Variations:*

- Have the participants brainstorm ideas around a specific topic (e.g., "ways to make meetings more effective," "ways to cut costs").
- Have the participants name the steps of a process as review.
- Have the participants name customer characteristics or needs.
- Have the participants list their individual job responsibilities as a getting-to-know each other exercise.

*Tips:*

- Encourage the participants to keep talking, even if they repeat themselves or say something that doesn't make sense.
- Encourage the group to pass the object quickly, especially if it is a large group.
- This activity lends itself to any topic that can involve listing words or characteristics.

*Suggested Debrief Questions:*

- How do you feel compared to when we started?
- How did you censor yourself?
- Why was this energizing?
- What is the value of passing the object?

*Source:*

- Chicago City Limits.

# Invisible Balls

*Overview:*
- In a circle, participants throw invisible balls accompanied by sounds. The first person tosses the ball and makes a sound. The receiver catches the ball and mimics the same sound. He then throws the ball to another person, making a new sound, which is repeated by the receiver. Eventually, more than one ball can be passed around the circle at the same time.

*Improv Topic:*
- Trust
- Spontaneity
- Accepting offers
- Listening and awareness
- Nonverbal behavior

*Purpose:*
- Icebreaker
- Warm-up
- Energy builder
- Team building
- Creativity
- Communication

*Supplies:*
- Invisible balls (none)

*Time:*
- 5–20 minutes

*Number of Players:*
- 4–20 per group

*Game Flow:*
- Form a circle.
- Explain that you have an invisible ball. Toss it to someone and have him or her catch it. Then have them throw it back to you.
- Further explain that the ball makes sound. This time throw the ball with a sound. "Wheee." Coach the receiver to repeat the sound.

- Have that person throw the ball to someone else, making a new sound, which is echoed by the receiver, and so on.
- After the group has tossed the ball for a while, ask for feedback— "How do you feel?" "Anyone censoring themselves?" "Why?" (See page 29 for a detailed description.)
- Continue the game adding more balls.
- Debrief.

*Variations:*
- Play with words instead of sounds.
- Play with sensory images (e.g., the smell of grass, a wet puppy tongue licking my face).
- Play with shared images—one person throws the first half, and the second catches the completion (e.g., Person A: "A really high skyscraper . . ." Person B: . . . "with a gorilla standing on the top.").
- Play with the thrower mouthing the words and the receiver articulating out loud what they understood the first person to say.

*Tips:*
- Keep up a fast pace. Speed will help participants bypass their censors.
- Be willing to play along and make silly or ordinary sounds yourself.

*Suggested Debrief Questions:*
- Are you censoring yourselves? How? What were some of the judgments you made?
- Did anyone plan his or her sounds ahead of time? Why?
- Did anyone compare their sounds to other people's sounds?
- What does this tell us about our tendencies to censor in real life?
- How does this relate to creativity and idea generation?
- How did your experience change as the game continued?
- How did your experience change as more balls were added?

*Source:*
- Adapted from Viola Spolin, Chicago City Limits, Fratelli Bologna, Theatresports, and Patricia Ryan.

# Neutral Status Scene

*Overview:*
- Participants are given a short script of 8–10 lines of neutral dialogue. The scene may be completely neutral or depict a job interview or coaching session. (See the following sample scene.) Pairs take turns enacting the scene, playing with the status relationships through their nonverbal choices. The rest of the group observes.

*Improv Topic:*
- Nonverbal behavior
- Listening and awareness
- Storytelling

*Purpose:*
- Team building
- Communication

*Supplies:*
- Handouts, flip chart, or slide with the scene recorded

*Time:*
- 15–30 minutes

*Number of Players:*
- Pairs

*Game Flow:*
- Hand out or post the scene.
- Recruit two volunteers to act it out.
- Allow the participants to play the scene without any outside direction once.
- Discuss the perceived status of each character.
- Assign status roles to each player and have them play the scene again. Combinations can include
  - Person A is high, Person B is low.
  - Person B is high, Person A is low.
  - Both are high.
  - Both are low.

- Status remains equal but shifts.
- Status switches—one starts high and ends low, the other starts low and ends high.
- Substitute the two players with others and continue to try different combinations.
- Discuss as you go.
- Debrief.

*Variations:*
- Use one pair to demo and then divide participants into trios to practice—two actors and one observer.
- Have the group write their own neutral scene.
- Set up status battles where the observers vote on who is the lowest or the highest.
- Add 30 seconds of silence somewhere in the scene.
- Allow teams to improvise scenes in their own words.

*Tips:*
- Sample Scene: The Job Interview
  A: Good morning.
  B: Good morning.
  A: Have a seat.
  B: Thank you.
  A: I have looked over your resume.
  B: Yes?
  A: I see you worked at Global, Inc.
  B: Yes. For a number of years.
  A: Very impressive.
  B: Thanks.
- If you have the participants create the scene, make sure the dialogue really feels neutral.
- Allow one team to try a couple of different status interactions before moving on to the next team.
- Feel free to freeze the action of the scene in the middle to point out an especially clear status moment.
- Be aware that attempts to claim status can backfire. High-status people can fall quickly if the other person fails to be intimidated, and low-status people can gain status by being too self-focused.

*Suggested Debrief Questions:*
- How much do you think the words mattered in this interaction?
- What were the most effective ways to raise your status?
- What lowered status?
- What status choices would you like to make in a real-life interview? A sales call? A coaching session?
- What is the value of being aware of status behavior in general?

*Source:*
- Adapted from Keith Johnstone's *Impro*, and Freestyle Repertory Theatre.

# One–Sided Scene

*Overview:*
- Two participants role play an interaction. One of them can speak. The other may only respond nonverbally.

*Improv Topic:*
- Nonverbal behavior
- Listening and awareness
- Accepting offers

*Purpose:*
- Team building
- Communication

*Supplies:*
- None

*Time:*
- 3–5 minutes per role play

*Number of Players:*
- Pairs

*Game Flow:*
- Ask for two volunteers.
- Assign a scenario (e.g., a job interview, a coaching session, an interview with a reporter, a father and son driving home from school, etc.) and an objective or goal for one of the participants.
- Allow that participant to speak. The other must react and respond naturally, but without using any words.
- Role-play the interaction until the objective is achieved or until time runs out.

*Variations:*
- Play half the scenario with one person speaking and then switch in the middle.
- Call out which person may speak and switch back and forth at various intervals.
- Play in concurrent groups, with two participants and one or two observers in each group.

- Role-play the scenario completely silently, with neither participant speaking.
- Allow the nonspeaking participant to have two or three words that she can repeat (e.g., "yes," "sure," "I thought so." "Is that right?").

*Tips:*
- Coach the nonspeaking participant to act as naturally as possible, finding some justification for not speaking. Remind them not to mime or exaggerate their behavior as in charades.
- Coach the speaker to notice and accept the offers that his partner is making. Is he giving in? Is he objecting? Has he agreed?
- The objectives or goals should involve the other person (e.g., "Get her to give me the job." "Convince him to come to work on time." "Let my son know I'm getting a divorce without having him hate me.").

*Suggested Debrief Questions:*
- What kind of signals did you get from your partner's nonverbal behavior?
- How easy was it to read his reactions?
- When did you find yourself paying attention to his facial expressions and body? When did you ignore them?
- Nonspeakers, how involved did you feel? How much of an effect did you feel you were able to have?
- Observers, how easy was it for you to read the nonspeakers?
- How did you feel when you saw something that the speaker did not seem to respond to?
- Speakers, did you know when you had met your objective?
- What did you do when you felt your tactics weren't working?
- How can we use this type of awareness in real life?

*Source:*
- Adapted from Chicago City Limits.

# One-Word-at-a-Time Exercises

*Overview:*
- A variety of foundational exercises that are ubiquitous in the improv community. A number of participants narrate a story or answer questions, each contributing only one word each turn.

*Improv Topic:*
- Spontaneity
- Accepting offers
- Listening and awareness
- Storytelling

*Purpose:*
- Warm-up
- Energy builder
- Team building
- Creativity
- Communication
- Review

*Supplies:*
- None

*Time:*
- 5–30 minutes

*Number of Players:*
- 2–20

*Game Flow:*
- Have participants stand in a circle.
- Provide a topic or title for a story.
- Tell the story, with each successive person contributing the next word.

*Variations:*
- Tell a story two words at a time.
- Tell a story with each person adding one word the first time around the circle, then two words, then three, then four, in successive passes

around the circle. Then go back down: three words, two, and finally one, ending the story when it is the last person's turn to say one word.

- Tell a word-at-a-time story in pairs.
- Tell a word-at-a-time story in pairs, acting out the action of the story as you go.
- Create a word-at-a-time talk show, on which a host interviews a word-at-a-time expert (see "Expert Interviews," page 164).
- Create word-at-a-time "proverbs," which summarize the learning of the day. (One way to do this is to give each person in the circle only one turn so that the proverb must end with the last person.)

*Tips:*
- Remind the participants that there is no such thing as a small word; *a* and *the* are as necessary to the sense of the sentence as *dogsled* or *restructuring*.
- Participants can end a sentence with the inflection of their voice.
- Encourage eye contact.
- Encourage speed.

*Suggested Debrief Questions:*
- When did you feel satisfied? When were you frustrated?
- Did you censor yourself? How?
- Why did I encourage us to go quickly?
- What would happen if we did this every day for a year?
- How is this like teamwork on the job?

*Source:*
- Viola Spolin, Keith Johnstone, Chicago schools, Theatresports.

# Paired Drawing

*Overview:*

- In pairs, participants draw a face or other picture, alternating one line or feature at a time. Then they title it one letter at a time. (See page 58 for examples.)

*Improv Topic:*

- Spontaneity
- Accepting offers
- Nonverbal behavior

*Purpose:*

- Team building
- Creativity
- Communication

*Supplies:*

- Colored pens and paper, flip chart

*Time:*

- 10–20 minutes

*Number of Players:*

- Pairs

*Game Flow:*

- Distribute pens and paper.
- Explain that the task will be for each pair to draw a face, alternating one line or feature at a time.
- As soon as someone hesitates, the drawing is finished.
- Then the pair will title the drawing, alternating letters, until one person hesitates.
- Ask for a volunteer and model the activity.
- Allow the pairs to draw a few faces or move on to another picture that they wish to draw.
- Display the results.
- Debrief the process and the products.

*Variations:*
- Leave the subject of the drawing open.
- Pass the drawings around a circle or in groups of 3–5 participants.
- Have the entire group create a mural.

*Tips:*
- Be aware that participants will be influenced by your model. Say, "Now your face doesn't have to look anything like mine."
- Coach pairs to keep going if they seem to be hesitating and then continuing to draw.
- Coach pairs to work silently.

*Suggested Debrief Questions:*
- How was that process?
- Were there any moments when you censored yourself?
- Were there any moments when you objected to your partner's offer?
- What do you think of the results?
- How do these pictures compare to the drawings you think we would have created individually?
- What are the advantages to collaboration?
- What are the disadvantages?
- How is this like the kind of teamwork you experience on the job?

*Source:*
- Originally taken from Johnstone's "Eyes" exercise. Adaptations by Creative Advantage, Dan Klein, Bay Area Theatresports, and Fratelli Bologna.

# Picture Math

*Overview:*
- Participants work in groups of three. The person in the middle is in the "hot seat." The participant on their right asks them to describe imaginary pictures in a photo album. The third participant intersperses simple math problems for the participant in the "hot seat" to solve at the same time.

*Improv Topic:*
- Spontaneity
- Accepting offers
- Listening and awareness
- Storytelling

*Purpose:*
- Warm-up
- Energy builder
- Creativity

*Supplies:*
- None

*Time:*
- 10–15 minutes

*Number of Players:*
- 3 per group

*Game Flow:*
- Split the participants into triads. (If there are leftover people, create groups of four, with one observer for each round.)
- Ask them to stand in a horseshoe.
- The person in the middle is in the "hot seat." He opens an imaginary picture album.
- The person on his right is in charge of asking him to describe the pictures in the album (e.g., "Who is that?" "What is she wearing?" "Where is that place?" "What is that painting in the background?").
- The person on his left periodically asks *simple* addition and subtraction problems simultaneously, using the previous answer as

the first number of the next problem (e.g., "3 plus 3" . . . "minus two" . . . "plus 10"). This requires the middle player to both do math and remember the previous number.

- After a few minutes the participants switch, until each person has played each role.

*Variations:*
- Ask the person on the right to interview the participant rather than describe pictures.
- Ask the participant to describe the pictures in rhyme.

*Tips:*
- Model the activity before it begins.
- Coach the individuals asking questions not to provide too much information (e.g., ask "Who is that?" not "Who is that woman sitting in the rocking chair with the blue wig?").
- Coach that person to switch the topic or turn the page if the "hot seat" person seems to be getting too comfortable.
- Remind the individuals asking the math problems to keep them simple. The activity is difficult enough.
- The math problems should be asked at intervals that keep the "hot seat" person on her toes, but allow her to spend some time focusing on the imaginary pictures.
- Coach the person in the middle to keep talking until interrupted with a math problem and then go right back to describing the picture.
- Coach her to say a number quickly and move on, even if she is not sure that she is right.

*Suggested Debrief Questions:*
- What do you think is going on in this exercise? (We are working our conscious rational mind to distract it from interfering with our creative impulses. We are also stimulating our brains visually, orally, aurally, artistically, and rationally all at the same time. This game is a virtual brain gym.)
- How many found it harder to do the math? How many found it harder to describe the pictures?
- Did your descriptions surprise you?

- What did you notice while you were asking questions? Math problems?
- What images do you remember?

*Source:*
- Adapted from Chicago City Limits.

# Picture Poetry

*Overview:*
- In pairs, participants describe an imaginary picture in verse.

*Improv Topic:*
- Spontaneity
- Accepting offers
- Listening and awareness
- Storytelling

*Purpose:*
- Warm-up
- Team building
- Creativity
- Communication

*Supplies:*
- None

*Time:*
- 4–10 minutes

*Number of Players:*
- Pairs

*Game Flow:*
- Divide the participants into pairs.
- Ask for one pair to volunteer to demonstrate.
- Instruct the two participants to imagine that they are viewing a picture in a gallery.
- Have the first person offer a sentence describing the picture.
- Have the second person offer a second sentence that rhymes with the first. Then have him offer a third line.
- The first person rhymes with that line and offers another that does not rhyme, and so forth.
- Continue for two minutes or until the picture seems complete.
- Have the rest of the participants engage in the activity simultaneously.

*Variations:*
- Have the participants describe the picture without rhyming.
- Play with three to five participants.
- Have the participants tell a story or describe an event in rhyme.

*Tips:*
- Rhyming is easier than it seems. If the participants are nervous, you can warm them up by shouting out a word and having the entire group shout back a rhyming word simultaneously. You may also coach participants to say a nonsense word if they cannot think of an actual word that rhymes.
- Coach the participants to go fast, so that they do not fall victim to their censors.
- Provide a suggestion for the type of picture the pairs are looking at if they feel stuck.

*Suggested Debrief Questions:*
- How did it feel to rhyme?
- What kind of picture did you describe?
- What surprised you about what you created?
- How well did you work together?
- What was difficult? What was easy?
- What is the value of rhyming? (We make offers to ourselves when we rhyme. Being forced to come up with a rhyme, prompts us to think outside the box, as well as to do more than one thing at the same time—a great way to bypass our censors.)

*Source:*
- Michael Gelman, the Chicago improv schools.

# Safety Zone

*Overview:*
- Participants secretly pick enemies and bodyguards and attempt to keep their bodyguards between them and their enemies.

*Improv Topic:*
- Spontaneity
- Accepting offers
- Nonverbal behavior

*Purpose:*
- Warm-up
- Energy builder
- Team building

*Supplies:*
- None

*Time:*
- 3–6 minutes

*Number of Players:*
- 8–100

*Game Flow:*
- Ask each participant to look around the room and privately decide on one other person whom they will consider Person A.
- Then ask them to pick another person, again secretly, and label that person, Person B.
- Inform them that Person A is their enemy and Person B is their bodyguard. The goal is to make sure that your guard is between you and your enemy at all times.
- Before people start to move, remind them to walk and that no one should get hurt.
- Play two or three rounds, choosing new enemies and bodyguards each time.

*Variations:*
- Call the game "Eclipse" and use the words *sun* and *moon* rather than *enemy* and *guard*.

- As a final round, make each person play the role of guard, so that Person A remains the enemy, but Person B becomes the person to be protected. The job of the participants, then, is to stay in between A and B.

*Tips:*
- The process will result in a wild, swirling pattern. Continue to remind people to walk. This activity is significantly more fun than it appears on paper.
- The last variation will result in a tight clump of people.
- Check for physical limitations before playing the game and remind people to WALK not run.

*Suggested Debrief Questions:*
- What happened?
- How do you feel? Why are you laughing?
- What feels different now?
- What is the value of physical activity?

*Source:*
- Theatresports, Freestyle Repertory Theatre, and Diane Rachel.

# Slap Pass

*Overview:*
- The participants stand in a circle. Someone claps their hands in the direction of someone else. That person passes the clap along to someone else, and so forth. The game should go very quickly.

*Improv Topic:*
- Spontaneity
- Listening and awareness
- Accepting offers
- Trust
- Nonverbal behavior
- Storytelling

*Purpose:*
- Warm-up
- Energy builder
- Team building
- Creativity
- Communication

*Supplies:*
- None

*Time:*
- 5–15 minutes

*Number of Players:*
- 5–25

*Game Flow:*
- Have the participants stand in a circle.
- One person claps at another, making eye contact and pointing his hand in her direction.
- That person claps at the next person, and so on, randomly around the circle.

*Variations:*
- Participants clap in order around the circle, gradually speeding up until the clap is going around the circle as fast as possible.

- Participants pass the clap around the circle, clapping in pairs simultaneously, so that Person A and Person B clap together, then B and C, then C and D, and so forth. The goal is to increase the speed and at the same time, clap exactly in unison.
- Participants clap around the circle, but can change direction whenever they wish, passing the clap back around the other way. This is a good game for discussing patterns. (See chapter 6 on Storytelling.)
- Participants clap around the circle and can change directions. When they are clapping to the right, they clap once. When they are clapping to the left they clap twice.

*Tips:*
- The original version of the game is a wonderful warm-up, energy-generator, and spontaneity exercise.
- The other more complicated versions are good for beginning discussions on storytelling, specifically pattern creation and reincorporation. After teaching the game, coach participants to look for patterns and try to repeat them. You may also ask a group to tell a story with claps.
- In the versions of the game that permit changing direction, you may tell the group that changing direction is making a new offer. Continuing in the same direction is accepting an offer. Debrief the effect of each choice.
- Coach participants not to talk during the exercise.
- Coach participants to make their partners look good—no faking them out (i.e., Don't look at one person and clap at another).

*Suggested Debrief Questions:*
- What kinds of stories did you make up based on the clap patterns?
- What helped us go faster?
- How do you feel compared to when we began?
- How does this relate to collaboration and communication in the workplace?

*Source:*
- Theatresports.

# Speaking in Unison

*Overview:*
- Groups of three to five participants tell a story, answer questions, or explain a process in unison, vocally mirroring each other.

*Improv Topic:*
- Spontaneity
- Accepting offers
- Listening and awareness
- Storytelling

*Purpose:*
- Warm-up
- Energy builder
- Team building
- Creativity
- Communication
- Review

*Supplies:*
- None

*Time:*
- 3–5 minutes per group

*Number of Players:*
- 3–5 per group

*Game Flow:*
- Recruit three to five volunteers.
- Give them a title for a story.
- Instruct them to speak in one voice, as if they were one person.
- Ask them a few simple questions to get them warmed up and then let them proceed to tell the story (e.g., What is your name? How did you get here today?).
- Coach with questions along the way if necessary.
- Have groups try it in front of the entire group or play simultaneously.

*Variations:*
- Have the participants role-play as a guest on a talk show and speak in unison as they answer questions. (See "Expert Interviews," page 164.)
- Have the participants explain a process or learning point.
- Have two groups of three to five participants each have a conversation in unison.

*Tips:*
- Remind the group that this is a very difficult task. They should expect to make mistakes.
- The trick to successfully speaking in unison is to mirror each other's mouth and "yes, and" the sounds and shapes. You may find that joining a group and helping them along is beneficial.
- Encourage groups to go as fast as they can and still stay together.
- Encourage members of the group to share leadership—both initiating and following.
- If a sentence doesn't make sense, or the group members get out of sync, ask them to repeat what they just said.
- The interviewing versions are easier than the longer narrative versions. Choose a format that the group is comfortable with.

*Suggested Debrief Questions:*
- What enables us to complete this task?
- How much did you feel the group shared leadership?
- How much did you initiate?
- How often did you follow?
- When were you most comfortable?
- What does this activity tell us about collaboration?

*Source:*
- Keith Johnstone, Freestyle Repertory Theatre.

# Speech Tag

*Overview:*
- In groups of three or four, participants tell a story, tagging each other when they want to take over the narrative.

*Improv Topic:*
- Spontaneity
- Accepting offers
- Listening and awareness
- Storytelling
- Nonverbal behavior

*Purpose:*
- Team building
- Creativity
- Communication
- Review

*Supplies:*
- None

*Time:*
- 3–5 minutes per group

*Number of Players:*
- 3–5 per group

*Game Flow:*
- Ask for three to five volunteers.
- Have one person stand in front with the others behind them in a horseshoe.
- Give the group a suggestion of something to talk about—a story title, a character or product name, a technical process.
- Have the person in front begin to talk. After a bit, have the second person tag them out (tap them on the shoulder) and continue the story exactly where the first person left off.
- Have the other participants randomly tag in and continue the story until it is finished, all the participants tagging in when they feel they want to or their partner needs to be relieved.
- Continue until the story is done.

*Variations:*
- Have the players take over in order.
- Have each player tag in only once, ending the story with the last player.
- Have the players speak in rhyme.
- Have the players tell the story as a monologue, taking on the same character body and voice. (This version is especially good for nonverbal behavior discussions.)
- Instruct the players when to switch, calling out their names or pointing to them. (See "Conducted Narrative," page 153.)

*Tips:*
- Coach the players to tag in, even if they do not know what they are going to say, especially if their partner looks like he needs help.
- Coach the players to increase the speed with which they tag in.
- Coach the players to start speaking exactly where their partner left off.

*Suggested Debrief Questions:*
- When did you choose to jump in?
- When did you hesitate?
- What was difficult? What was enjoyable?
- What kind of offers were there to accept?
- What were you thinking about while you were not speaking?
- How do you feel about what you created as a group?

*Source:*
- Freestyle Repertory Theatre, Chicago improv schools.

# Spontaneous Marketing

*Overview:*
- In groups, participants brainstorm a name, logo, tagline, and ad campaign.

*Improv Topic:*
- Spontaneity
- Accepting offers

*Purpose:*
- Icebreaker
- Team building
- Creativity
- Communication

*Supplies:*
- Flip charts (1 per group)
- Markers

*Time:*
- 15–20 minutes, plus 3 minutes per group to share

*Number of Players:*
- 2–5 per group

*Game Flow:*
- Divide the participants into equal groups of 2–5 participants and provide each one with a flip chart and markers.
- Tell them that they have 12 minutes to come up with the following for marketing themselves as a group:
  - A name
  - A logo
  - A tagline
  - An ad campaign (e.g., a TV commercial that shows. . . .; a billboard that has Barney on it and says. . . .).
- At 3-minute intervals, remind them to move on to the next topic if they haven't already.
- Require that every member of the group be involved in the presentation of the results.
- Have each group present its "pitch."

*Variations:*
- Have each group pitch a topic or product from the training.
- Have each group improvise their pitch—each participant throws out an idea, and the rest of the group builds on it without planning.
- Have groups create a poem or song that describes their group.
- Have groups create a secret handshake.

*Tips:*
- Enforcing short-ish time limits helps the creative process. If people feel that they did not have enough time, that does two things: gives them an excuse to not be brilliant and honors their spontaneous responses without overevaluating.
- Walk around as the groups are working and encourage them to accept ideas.
- You may wish to run the activity as a contest and judge on creativity and participation. If you do, it is possible to have the results be a tie or to have prizes for each team. The payoff of framing as a contest may be increased motivation. The price for having one winner may be a reduced level of comfort being spontaneous or creative.

*Suggested Debrief Questions:*
- How did the process go in your individual groups?
- Were there things that would have made you feel more comfortable or successful as individuals? How about as a team?
- What did you especially enjoy?
- How do you feel about the results?
- How would they have been different if you had been working alone?
- What is the value of collaboration versus individual creativity?
- What did you learn about the creative process?

*Source:*
- Adapted from Viola Spolin and Del Close's "Ad Game."

# Stats

*Overview:*
- A musical chairs–like game, in which participants exchange tidbits of information about themselves and find out what they have in common.

*Improv Topic:*
- Trust
- Spontaneity

*Purpose:*
- Icebreaker
- Warm-up
- Energy builder
- Team building
- Communication
- Needs assessment

*Supplies:*
- One chair per participant

*Time:*
- 15–30 minutes

*Number of Players:*
- 6–20 per circle

*Game Flow:*
- Arrange a circle of chairs, one for each participant.
- Stand in the center of the circle.
- State the following rules:
  - Whoever is standing in the center shouts out the next "stat."
  - Each statistic must be true of the person who says it.
  - If that statistic is true of you, find a new chair.
  - NO ONE GETS HURT.
- Offer the first statistic.
- Play along. (If you are not playing, make sure there is one fewer chair than participants, and have one volunteer start in the middle.)
- Play for however long you wish. You may give a three-minute or three-round warning if you like.

*Variations:*

- Use as a needs-analysis or more focused content activity by setting parameters around the types of statements (e.g., the statements must involve sales experiences; the statements must be about your experiences with diversity).
- If you have a very large group or a space that will not accommodate a circle of chairs, you may play "Roaming Stats." For this version:
  - Follow the general rules, but instead of having the participants find new chairs, have the speaker instruct participants to go to a certain part of the room (e.g., over in the corner; behind the table; at the far wall).
  - Whoever wishes to shout out the next statistic is free to do so.
  - Additional advantages to this version are:
    - The group can see who fits into each category more easily.
    - It is less physically demanding.
    - The flow is more free-form, so that anyone with an idea has the opportunity to shout it out.

*Tips:*

- Check with participants about any physical limitations. I have had participants on crutches or in wheelchairs play by touching the chair with a hand or crutch. And pregnant women have enjoyed the game, too. Still you must get buy-in ahead of time.

*Suggested Debrief Questions:*

- What did you find out that surprised you?
- What did you share that surprised you?
- What is the value of playing this game?
- Why do we censor ourselves?
- What would you like to change about your interactions based on this experience?

*Source:*

- Bay Area Theatresports, Ruth Zapora, and Patricia Ryan.

# Status Cards

*Overview:*
- Participants are given a playing card that indicates their status. Each participant "wears" their card on their forehead without knowing what is on the card. As if they are at an annual employee meeting, the participants treat each other with the status indicated by the card. At the end of the role play, the group lines up in order of their perceived status.

*Improv Topic:*
- Nonverbal behavior
- Listening and awareness

*Purpose:*
- Warm-up
- Energy builder
- Team building
- Communication

*Supplies:*
- 1 deck of cards for every 52 people

*Time:*
- 10–20 minutes

*Number of Players:*
- 5–100

*Game Flow:*
- Distribute a playing card to each participant. Make sure that there is a variety of numbers—low to high.
- Instruct the participants not to look at their cards as you pass them out.
- Have the group place the cards face out on their foreheads, still without looking at their own cards.
- Set up a role play. Explain that the group is at an annual company meeting. Each person should be treated with the status indicated by his card. (Aces are high; twos are low.) As the players get clues about

their status, they should take on the behaviors that are associated with it.

- After a few minutes of mingling, ask the participants to form a line with the lowest card at one end and the highest at the other. Participants should place themselves where they think they belong, still refraining from looking at their own cards.
- If there are fewer than 20 players, ask each one to guess their card out loud.
- Invite the players to look at their cards.
- Debrief.

*Variations:*
- Set up a different scenario for the role play (e.g., an office party; an awards ceremony; Santa's workshop at the North Pole; a board meeting).
- Play without words.
- Play more than one round, so that each person gets to experience more than one position.
- Play a round in which people see their own card and not the others.
- Play a round in which everyone sees all the cards.

*Tips:*
- Status is touchy. Leave lots of time for discussion.
- You may wish to play "Status Demo" or "Status Pass" before this activity to introduce the concept of status and illustrate high- and low-status behaviors.
- You may wish to follow up with "Neutral Status Scene."
- Remind people many times to refrain from looking at their cards.

*Suggested Debrief Questions:*
- What kind of signals did you get as to your status?
- What kind of signals did you give?
- How did it feel to be very high? Very low? In the middle?
- Who were you most comfortable talking to?
- What assumptions did you make about people with different statuses?

- Those of you who did not guess your cards, why not? What signals did you get? What internal assumptions did you make?
- How did you feel when other people behaved in ways that contradicted their assigned status?
- How is this like real life?

*Source:*
- Adapted from Matt Smith, Rebecca Stockley, and Seattle Theatresports.

# Status Demo

*Overview:*

- Participants mingle, as if at a party, with half of the group displaying high-status physical behaviors and the other half low-status behaviors. After a few minutes, the groups switch.

*Improv Topic:*

- Trust
- Status
- Nonverbal behavior
- Listening and awareness

*Purpose:*

- Warm-up
- Team building
- Communication

*Supplies:*

- None

*Time:*

- 5–15 minutes

*Number of Players:*

- 5–100

*Game Flow:*

- Split the group in two.
- Assign one group to take on the following high-status behaviors:
  - Take up as much space in the room as possible, physically and vocally.
  - Move smoothly.
  - Make eye contact and hold it comfortably.
  - Make (appropriate) physical contact directly and comfortably.
  - Hold your head still, but not stiff.
- Assign the other to take on the following low-status behaviors
  - Take up as little space as possible.
  - Say "um, and uh . . ." when you talk.
  - Touch your face and hair often.

- Try to make eye contact, but find it sort of painful.
- Want to make physical contact, but it kind of stings.
- Tell the two groups that they are at a party. They all know each other and are happy to be there. Have the groups mingle. Inform them that they may talk to anyone they wish, from either group.
- After a few minutes, have the participants switch status roles. Remind the group of the specific behaviors and have them mingle again.
- Debrief.

*Variations:*
- Do not tell the group that you are focusing on status. See what assumptions they make about the members of the other group.
- Assign just one behavior to each group and see how it informs the rest of their behaviors.
- If there are few enough participants, have them interact as if they were in a meeting.
- First have everyone take on high-status behaviors, and then low-status, before mixing the two.

*Tips:*
- Status is touchy. Leave time for discussion.
- "Status Pass," "Status Cards," and "Neutral Status Scene" are potential follow-up exercises. Each of them explores status in subtler ways than this activity.

*Suggested Debrief Questions:*
- How did you feel in each role?
- Was one more comfortable than the other?
- What assumptions did you make about the other folks?
- Who were you more comfortable talking to?
- What happens to communication as the status gap grows?
- How much does our physicality affect status in real life?
- How else is this exercise a reflection of the real world?
- What are some examples of status interactions in your jobs?

*Source:*
- Keith Johnstone, Bay Area Theatresports, and Fratelli Bologna.

# Status Pass

*Overview:*
- The participants stand in a circle and take turns, verbally or nonverbally, lowering and then raising the status of the person to their right.

*Improv Topic:*
- Trust
- Nonverbal behavior

*Purpose:*
- Warm-up
- Team building
- Communication

*Supplies:*
- None

*Time:*
- 5–15 minutes

*Number of Players:*
- 2–20 per group

*Game Flow:*
- Have participants stand in a circle.
- Instruct the first person to turn to her right and lower the status of the next person with a phrase or gesture.
- That person does the same, and so on around the circle.
- Then have the first person raise her partner's status, and continue through the rest of the group.

*Variations:*
- Raise and lower status with nonverbal behavior only.
- Play in pairs, trading back and forth.
- Assign a neutral line of dialogue to each participant.
- Instruct the participants to decide privately whether they wish to raise or lower their partner's status and then have the rest of the group guess their intention.

*Tips:*
- It is important to lower status first, and then raise it, so that participants are left feeling validated, not dismissed.
- "Status Cards" and "Neutral Status Scene" are potential follow-up activities.

*Suggested Debrief Questions:*
- How did it feel to deliberately lower someone's status?
- How often do we unconsciously have our status lowered, or lower others'?
- How did it feel to have your status lowered? Raised?
- How can being conscious of the large impact of these subtle interactions help us?

*Source:*
- Adapted from Keith Johnstone and Chicago City Limits.

# Story Exchange

*Overview:*
- Participants exchange short stories from their lives. After exchanging stories, they cycle through a number of rounds in which they tell the stories they have just heard, as if they were their own. Finally, the group comes together in a circle, and each member again tells the last story they have heard. Think a giant, complex game of telephone.

*Improv Topic:*
- Listening and awareness
- Storytelling
- Trust
- Accepting offers
- Nonverbal behavior

*Purpose:*
- Icebreaker
- Team building
- Creativity
- Communication

*Supplies:*
- 3"x5" cards
- Pens

*Time:*
- 25–50 minutes

*Number of Players:*
- 10–20

*Game Flow:*
- Pass out 3"x5" cards and pens.
- Assign participants a number and have them write it on their card, as big and as legibly as possible.
- Have the participants find a partner and decide who will be an A and who will be a B.
- Have the As tell the Bs a story from their life. The stories should be:
  - True.

- About 60–90 seconds long.
- From any period or aspect of their lives (e.g., something that happened this week, something that happened in childhood).
- The Bs should LISTEN ONLY. They should not interrupt or ask questions.
- When the As finish, have the Bs tell a story.
- Have the partners exchange their cards. Each person now has the card with the number of the story they just heard.
- Ask everyone to find a new partner.
- Each person now tells the story THAT SHE JUST HEARD, in the first person ("*I* took the goldfish . . .") as accurately as possible, as if it is her story. Stress that each participant is to attempt to tell the story exactly as she heard it. (Note: Hold off telling the participants that they will have to repeat their partners' stories until this point.)
- When both participants have told their stories, ask them to exchange their cards and find a new partner.
- This time, ask people to make sure that they are not paired with someone who has a card with a number they have already seen. This process ensures that no one will get their own story back or hear the same story more than once.
- Again, have the participants exchange stories and swap cards.
- Have the participants form a circle and one by one tell the story that they just heard.

*Variations:*
- Assign a specific topic for the stories (e.g., a story involving technology; a story from childhood; a management experience).
- Demo Version (This version is good for use with large groups, when having each person tell a story would be unwieldy, and also useful for allowing participants to view the process of the stories changing and track how the changes occur.):
  - Ask for four volunteers (A, B, C, and D).
  - Send C and D out of the room.
  - Have A tell a story to B.
  - Then C reenters, and B tells the story she just heard from A.
  - Then D reenters, and C tells D A's story, as told by B.

- Finally, D retells A's story to the group at large.
- Debrief.

*Tips:*
- Refrain from discussion of the changes in the stories until everyone has shared.
- Let the individuals volunteer to go next, rather than going in order around the circle. This will help to keep the entire group engaged.

*Suggested Debrief Questions:*
- How did we do?
- Did anyone not recognize his or her story?
- What kinds of changes were there in your stories?
- What sorts of things can you listen for (facts, feelings, intentions)?
- What was your experience of listening to the stories?
- How did your experience change when you knew you would have to repeat the story you were hearing?
- How can we become more skilled listeners?

*Source:*
- Adapted from Viola Spolin and Theatresports.

# Story of Your Name

*Overview:*
- Participants share the story of how they got their names.

*Improv Topic:*
- Trust
- Storytelling

*Purpose:*
- Icebreaker
- Warm-up
- Team building
- Communication

*Supplies:*
- None

*Time:*
- Approximately 1–2 minutes per participant

*Number of Players:*
- Variable

*Game Flow:*
- Have each participant share the story of his or her name.
- Let them know that they can tell the story of their first name, last name, a nickname, whatever they like.
- Some facilitators like to add that participants can lie if they wish. This takes the onus off of people who do not wish to share, or feel as if they do not have a story to tell.
- Model the process by going first.
- Let the speaker pick the next speaker.

*Variations:*
- If the group is too large for everyone to participate in the allotted amount of time, split the group into subgroups. Subgroups of 6–10 are ideal.

*Tips:*
- Set a time limit of one minute if you have a large group or not a lot of time. Folks will find they can talk about themselves for a long time.
- If someone says they have absolutely no story about their name, you might prompt them to talk about how they feel about their name, or what name they wanted to have as a child.

*Suggested Debrief Questions:*
- What is the value of learning non-work-related information about each other?
- Did you discover anything about yourself that you didn't know?
- What did you learn about the group in general?
- In what ways do you feel different from before we began the exercise?
- What effect does hearing a personal story have?
- How does it feel to share a personal story?

*Source:*
- Bay Area Theatresports, via George Silides's icebreaking activities for pastors.

# Story Seeds

*Overview:*
- The facilitator or group members come up with four neutral sentences. Then, individually, they write stories encompassing those four sentences, but adding characterizations and details.

*Improv Topic:*
- Storytelling
- Accepting offers

*Purpose:*
- Creativity
- Communication
- Needs assessment
- Problem solving
- Review

*Supplies:*
- Pens and paper

*Time:*
- 10–20 minutes

*Number of Players:*
- Variable

*Game Flow:*
- The facilitator presents four neutral sentences, or elicits them from the group (e.g., The manager walked into the call center. The lights flickered. Joe ate a sandwich. The computer froze.).
- Each individual writes a story or monologue incorporating those four sentences however they wish.
- Give the participants approximately 10 minutes to write their stories.
- Share as desired.

*Variations:*
- As a review activity, provide content words or models rather than sentences.
- As a problem-solving exercise, provide an objective in addition to the four sentences.

- Allow participants to work in pairs or teams.
- Provide a first and last sentence instead of four to be used at any point.

*Tips:*
- Some individuals are comfortable writing and working alone. Others are not. This activity can balance more collaborative and public activities.
- Do not force anyone to share what they have written.
- Give the participants the leeway to interpret the assignment however they wish. If they want to write a memo or dialogue, for example, let them. If they find themselves writing four separate small pieces, encourage them to follow their creative impulses.

*Suggested Debrief Questions:*
- What inspired you?
- How did you censor yourself?
- What did you especially enjoy in the stories you heard?
- What made these stories compelling?
- How could you use the process of writing to help you in other ways?

*Source:*
- Adapted from Kenn Adams and Freestyle Repertory Theatre.

# The Story Spine Story

*Overview:*
- Participants use this sentence-at-a-time template to create well-structured stories, individually or collaboratively. (See page 88 for discussion.)

*Improv Topic:*
- Storytelling
- Accepting offers
- Listening and awareness
- Spontaneity

*Purpose:*
- Warm-up
- Team building
- Creativity
- Communication
- Needs assessment
- Problem solving
- Review
- Closing

*Supplies:*
- A flip chart, slide, or handout with the Story Spine recorded

*Time:*
- 10–60 minutes

*Number of Players:*
- 1 to 5 per group

*Game Flow:*
- Present the Story Spine:
  - Once upon a time . . .
  - Every day . . .
  - But, one day, . . .
  - Because of that, . . . (Repeated three times, or as often as necessary)
  - Until finally . . .

- Ever since then . . .
- And the moral of the story is . . . (Optional)
- Have participants create a story one sentence at a time, using the cue words to begin each sentence.

*Variations:*
- The Story Spine can be used any time stories are incorporated into a design. For example:
  - As a review activity, divide the participants into groups and have them create a story that illustrates an important learning point.
  - Individually, have participants write the story of the workshop to assess learning, or before the workshop begins, as a way of assessing needs.
  - As a trainer, speaker, or presenter, use the Spine to create anecdotes or to hone existing ones.
  - As a visioning and problem-solving tool, the Story Spine can offer structure for brainstorming and action planning. (See "Story Visioning.")

*Tips:*
- Some people love structure, whereas others feel limited by it. Use the Story Spine merely as a support tool, allowing participants to deviate from it if they wish.
- If you are concentrating on storytelling, you may wish to analyze the structure (see chapter 6, page 86). Otherwise, the Story Spine can be presented as a tool without much explanation.

*Suggested Debrief Questions:*
- How did the structure help or hinder you?
- Was the process of creating a story easier or harder than you expected?
- What is the value of using stories in learning?
- What value does this structure provide?
- What are the other elements of good storytelling (details, emotion, presentation skills)?

*Source:*
- Originally created by Kenn Adams; adapted by StoryNet LLC.

# Story Visioning

*Overview:*
- Using the Story Spine (see previous activity), participants assume that their ideal vision of the future is the happy ending of a story. They then build a strategic plan, using the other narrative elements leading to that vision.

*Improv Topic:*
- Accepting offers
- Storytelling
- Trust

*Purpose:*
- Team building
- Creativity
- Communication
- Needs assessment
- Problem solving

*Supplies:*
- A flip chart and pens

*Time:*
- 30–60 minutes

*Number of Players:*
- 2–20

*Game Flow:*
- Agree on a vision. (See "Vision Weaving" as a possible activity.)
- Post the Story Spine. (See "The Story Spine Story" and chapter 6 for more details.)
  - Once upon a time . . .
  - Every day . . .
  - But, one day . . .
  - Because of that . . . (repeat as often as desired)
  - Until finally . . .
  - Ever since then, . . .
- Plug the vision into the "Ever since then" section.

- Tell the participants that "Once upon a time" is now. We are going to work on how to get from there to the end of the story, using the rest of the spine as a guide to creating an action plan.
- Have individuals create the story one sentence at a time around the circle. For the "because of that . . ." section, you may have each individual suggest how the person to their right contributed to achieving the happy ending.

*Variations:*
- Have individuals share or write their own version of the story, telling how they will personally contribute to the vision.
- Have groups of three to five participants create the vision story separately and then present to the group.
- Use the spine as a guide on a much larger scale, doing activities for the current state, strategic planning, and visioning.

*Tips:*
- Choose a format that maximizes the individual's involvement.
- Spend time forming and agreeing on a vision before you begin.
- Decide on the level of practicality that you are looking for. Is this an idea-generation session or a realistic problem-solving one?
- Make sure you are capturing all the ideas.

*Suggested Debrief Questions:*
- How was this process different from other visioning sessions?
- What felt right?
- What still feels troubling?
- How much of what we created feels possible?
- What do we still need to do?
- Has your picture of the future changed at all?
- How do you feel about your ability to personally affect the realization of the vision?

*Source:*
- StoryNet, LLC, based on Kenn Adams's Story Spine structure.

# True or False

*Overview:*
- Participants take turns telling one true story, and one false. The rest of the group guesses which is which.

*Improv Topic:*
- Listening and awareness
- Storytelling
- Nonverbal behavior

*Purpose:*
- Team building
- Creativity
- Communication

*Supplies:*
- None

*Time:*
- 15 minute preparation (or prep assigned ahead of time) plus 10 minutes per participant

*Number of Players:*
- Variable

*Game Flow:*
- Instruct each participant to think of a true story and a false story.
- Have the participants take turns telling both of their stories. The other members of the group guess which they think is the true story, and which is the false one.

*Variations:*
- Have three or four people tell stories, one of which is true. The observers guess which one it is.
- Have each participant think of a story and then come up with a one-sentence title or description (e.g., I once tried to buy a mink coat for $39). Then in groups of three or four, have the participants choose one of those titles that they wish to work with. Then, the person who

owns that title tells their story, while the others in the group tell made-up stories based on the same title. Observers guess which story is true.

- Play with real objects. So, each participant brings an object. The group decides on their favorite, and then each person tells the story of why that object is theirs—the real owner telling a true story, and the others making one up.

*Tips:*
- Encourage participants to create really false stories, rather than just changing minor details of a true one.
- In addition to discussing which stories were believable, you may choose to discuss which were most compelling. They may or may not be the same.
- You may choose whether to give people time to create stories ahead of time, or whether you wish them to plan in class, or improvise on the spot.

*Suggested Debrief Questions:*
- How easy was it to deceive people? Why?
- As observers, how did you decide which story was true?
- Did you have more fun telling true or made-up stories?
- What clues other than words did we receive as to the trustworthiness of the speaker?
- Which stories were most compelling? Were those mostly the true ones or not?
- Which qualities make a story compelling?
- How important is it that a story is true?
- What can you do if you want to make up a story to maintain credibility?

*Source:*
- General acting training.

# Vision Weaving

*Overview:*
- In a circle, participants create a sensory montage of their desired state. Individuals randomly shout out attributes of their ideal vision of the future. For example, "Customers tell their friends about our service." "Our stock has risen 300%." "We bring our dogs to work." "There is fresh bread baking in the kitchen."

*Improv Topic:*
- Trust
- Spontaneity
- Accepting offers
- Listening and awareness

*Purpose:*
- Warm-up
- Team building
- Creativity
- Communication
- Needs assessment
- Problem solving
- Closing

*Supplies:*
- A flip chart and pens or a tape recorder

*Time:*
- 10–20 minutes

*Number of Players:*
- 2–20

*Game Flow:*
- Seat the participants in a circle.
- Provide a specific focus for the vision (e.g., "our office in the year 2020" or "our organization one year from now").
- Tell the participants that in a minute you will ask them to close their eyes. You would like them to, at their leisure, offer details about their ideal vision of that environment.

- Tell them that anyone can say anything at any time, with the exception that no one may offer more than two ideas in a row.
- Remind them that they are not committed to any of the ideas stated, so that they should just let the suggestions wash over them without stopping to object or evaluate. There will be time for that later.
- Let them know that you may pepper the activity with questions.
- Begin.
- As the activity slows down naturally, tell the group that it is about to end. Ask if anyone has anything else they would like to add.
- Debrief.

*Variations:*
- Guide the image generation more specifically by offering scenarios and asking questions continuously (e.g., "You are in the lobby. You overhear two clients talking about your company. What do they say?").
- Have groups of two to five participants vision separately and then come together and share.
- Have individuals write down their individual visions and then swap papers randomly and share.

*Tips:*
- Coach the group to take its time and allow silence.
- Offer questions that spur the group to think about the following:
  - What do they see?
  - What do they hear (e.g., what people at work say; what they, themselves, say when they go home)?
  - What smells are in the air?
  - What are they able to do?
  - How do they feel?
- If there are a few members of the group who dominate, you may want to go around the circle in order for a while.
- To capture the vision, scribe or invite someone outside the group to do so. You may also choose to tape record the session for later transcription.
- Visioning sessions lead to change only when they are operationalized. Plan to use the information generated here in strategic planning activities.

*Suggested Debrief Questions:*
- How do you feel?
- How was that process?
- What do you think about that picture of the future?
- What elements really sparked your passion?
- What feels possible?
- What surprised you?
- Anything else you want to add?

*Source:*
- Rebecca Stockley and Michael Vance's "Five Sense Visioning" exercise.

# Warm-Up: Physical and Vocal

*Overview:*
- A general set of exercises for the voice and body to be done in a group setting or individually as ongoing conditioning or preparation for presentations.

*Improv Topic:*
- Nonverbal behavior
- Spontaneity
- Listening and awareness

*Purpose:*
- Icebreaker
- Warm-up
- Energy builder
- Communication

*Supplies:*
- None

*Time:*
- 7–10 minutes

*Number of Players:*
- 1–200

*Game Flow:*
- Have the participants stand in a circle in a grounded, neutral position—feet shoulder width apart, knees bent slightly, shoulders back and down, head loose and balanced, eyes straight ahead.
- Lead them through a series of slow stretches, head and shoulder rolls, and so forth. For example:
  - Stretch to each side, holding each position for a count of ten.
  - Roll the head gently around, remembering to lift it slightly in back so that the neck is not crunched.
  - Roll down the spine, so that you are hanging from the waist. Let your head drop. Shake out your shoulders and then slowly roll up, stacking each vertebra one on top of the next, bringing the head up last.

- Swing your arms back in the same direction for a count of eight, then forward, then one in one direction and one in the other.
- Shake out each leg and rotate the ankles, swing from the knees and then from the hips.
- Bend the knees and swing the hips back and forth, right and left, in circles.
- Isolate the rib cage and move it side-to-side, front and back, around in circles.
- Shake out the entire body.
- Lead the group through a series of vocal exercises. For example:
  - During the physical exercises just described, encourage the participants to breathe deeply from their diaphragm and to release sounds (ahhh, mmmm) as they exhale.
  - Massage the face and jaw. Make big faces, and scrunched faces.
  - Hum from the lowest part of the vocal register to the highest.
  - Blow through your lips.
  - Practice saying tongue twisters as clearly as possible.
  - Breathe in on a count of four, hold for four, breathe out for eight, hold empty for four. Work up to patterns of 8, 8, 16, 8, and then 16, 16, 32, 16.
  - Have the participants practice speaking to each other from across the room, so that they can be understood without shouting, but with strong supported voices.

*Variations:*
- There are a number of vocal training publications that can be consulted for more specific exercises and information.

*Tips:*
- People can feel vulnerable doing these kinds of drills. Make sure to model the exercises as you go, and acknowledge the risk.
- The more specific you can be as you lead the group, the safer they will feel.
- If anyone feels lightheaded, instruct them to take a break and have a seat.

*Suggested Debrief Questions:*
- How do you feel?

- What is the value of doing these kinds of warm-ups?
- What are two exercises that you can realistically see yourself incorporating into your real life?

*Source:*
- General acting training.

# Word Drill

*Overview:*
- This is a straightforward word-association game. In groups of three to five, participants take turns sitting in the "hot seat." The other participants shoot words at them, and they respond with the first word or phrase that comes to mind.

*Improv Topic:*
- Spontaneity
- Accepting offers
- Trust

*Purpose:*
- Warm-up
- Energy builder
- Creativity
- Communication

*Supplies:*
- None

*Time:*
- 6–12 minutes

*Number of Players:*
- 3 to 5 per group

*Game Flow:*
- Arrange the participants into groups of three to five.
- Ask one of them to stand facing the others, who form a horseshoe in front of them.
- One by one the other members of the group throw out a word. The person in the hot seat responds to each word with the first word or phrase that comes to mind. Then he fields the next word and responds.
- After a few minutes, the participants switch, and a new person takes the hot seat.

*Variations:*
- Play in pairs, shooting words back and forth.

- Play in a large group, with one person walking down the line of other participants, responding to a word from each one, and finally taking her place at the end of the line to participate in throwing out words for the next person.

*Tips:*
- Set up the activity as a content-less one. Assure them that the words they say will not be analyzed.
- Coach participants to respond as quickly as possible.
- Coach participants to respond without saying "um" or "uh."
- Coach the individuals who are giving words to shout them out as quickly as possible and to give unrelated words as much as possible, to keep the hot seat person off balance. Let the group know that their job is to provide that person with a workout, so the other individuals may think of their words ahead of time if they find that helps.
- Watch the participants to see when they seem "fried" and have them switch to the next person.

*Suggested Debrief Questions:*
- How did it feel to be in the hot seat?
- How did it feel to give words?
- How did you censor yourself?
- What happened as the exercise continued?
- How do you feel now?

*Source:*
- Matt Smith, Seattle improviser.

# Word Patterns

*Overview:*
- In a circle, the participants create a pattern of passing a word around the circle. Then they create a different pattern with a different word and pass both patterns simultaneously. Then a third pattern is added, and so on.

*Improv Topic:*
- Listening and awareness
- Trust
- Accepting offers

*Purpose:*
- Icebreaker
- Warm-up
- Energy builder
- Team building
- Communication

*Supplies:*
- None

*Time:*
- 15–20 minutes

*Number of Players:*
- 6–20

*Game Flow:*
- Have the participants stand in a circle.
- Point to someone across the circle and say, "You."
- That person puts her hand on her head to indicate that she has been pointed to, and then points to someone else across the circle. This process continues, until everyone has been incorporated into the pattern. The last person points back to you, the initiating facilitator.
- After the pattern has been established, have the participants repeat it a few times without the pointing, so that each person says "you" to the same person each time, passing the word through the pattern like a ball.
- Next initiate a new pattern, by pointing to a new person and saying something that falls into a category (e.g., animals, colors, HP

products, conflict resolution techniques). This time each person says a different word, but one that fits into the category.

- That new person puts his hand on his head to indicate that he has been pointed to, and then points to someone else across the circle. This pattern continues until everyone has been incorporated into it, with each person pointing to a different partner.
- Then both patterns are passed around the circle simultaneously.
- Continue to create and add a third and fourth pattern if the group is willing and able.

*Variations:*
- Create three patterns and then ask people to walk to their partner's place as they pass the original "you" pattern. This adds a level of difficulty because the layout of the circle will change.
- Start patterns without identifying a category, and have one emerge from the words that participants associate and add.
- Play with closed eyes.
- Play using the word *you* in the first pattern, *me* in the second, and *us* in the third.

*Tips:*
- Remember to check each pattern alone, before combining patterns.
- Remind participants to point to different people each time.
- Continue to pass the words through the circle more than once a round, to get momentum going when the group is doing well.
- Coach participants to take responsibility for their partners' receiving and passing along each word.

*Suggested Debrief Questions:*
- What did this feel like?
- What helped us achieve our task?
- What hindered us?
- What obstacles did we encounter?
- How did we help each other?
- How is this like collaborating in real life?

*Source:*
- Adapted from Theatresports worldwide, Carol Hazenfield.

# You're Out

*Overview:*
- Groups of participants role-play a meeting in which they compete to belong and exclude others from the group.

*Improv Topic:*
- Trust
- Nonverbal behavior
- Listening and awareness
- Storytelling
- Accepting offers

*Purpose:*
- Team building
- Communication

*Supplies:*
- None

*Time:*
- 3–5 minutes per scene

*Number of Players:*
- 3 participants per scene

*Game Flow:*
- Ask for three volunteers.
- Give them a setting for a role-play—a meeting, a holiday party, a grade school class.
- Instruct each person that their objective is to align themselves with someone and exclude the third person.
- Play the scene.
- Debrief.

*Variations:*
- Play so that one group rejects another group.
- Play so that one person rejects a group of others.
- Play with one person rejecting one other.

- Set specific scenarios, such as a trainer being rejected by workshop participants, a new hire being rejected by a team, a woman being rejected by her male counterparts at a bar.

*Tips:*
- This is an excellent exercise for exploring group dynamics. It is also very powerful. Be sure to create a safe space and debrief thoroughly. Ask the participants permission to play and let them know ahead of time what they will be doing.
- Play for short bits of time, changing participants often.
- The experience can be as revelatory for those watching as those playing. Make sure to include the observers in the debrief.

*Suggested Debrief Questions:*
- How did it feel to be excluded?
- How did it feel to belong?
- How did it feel to exclude?
- How did it feel to watch the scene?
- What techniques did you find for belonging?
- What behaviors led to exclusion?
- How do these dynamics play out in your workplace?

*Source:*
- Adapted from Viola Spolin's "Rejection" game and the work of Keith Johnstone, Diane Rachel, and Theatresports.

# ADDITIONAL ACTIVITIES

## Three Things in Common

*Overview:*
- In pairs, participants take one minute to find out three things they have in common that they didn't already know they had in common.

*Improv Topic:*
- Trust
- Spontaneity
- Listening and awareness
- Nonverbal behavior

*Purpose:*
- Icebreaker
- Team building
- Creativity
- Communication
- Needs assessment
- Energy builder
- Warm-up

*Supplies:*
- None

*Time:*
- 2–3 minutes per round

*Number of Players:*
- Pairs

*Game Flow:*
- In pairs, players find three things in common that they didn't previously know they had in common (e.g., "We are both men" doesn't count).
- They have one minute to accomplish the task.
- Do as many rounds as you wish, switching partners each time.

*Variations:*
- After the first round, have partners combine with another pair into groups of four and play again. Then into groups of eight.
- Have the pairs play without words.

*Tips:*
- Especially after the first round, encourage the pairs to take risks to share things they might not otherwise share.

*Suggested Debrief Questions:*
*(N.B.: as a warm-up game or energizer, you may find no extensive debrief necessary.)*
- What kind of things did you find you had in common?
- How was that? Do you feel closer to your partner now?
- What strategies did you use?
- What is the value of connecting in this way?

*Source:*
- BATS Improv, Rebecca Stockley.

# The 300-Year-Gap Conversation

*Overview:*
- In pairs, participant A attempts to communicate the use and value of a modern-day object to participant B, who plays the role of someone from 300 years ago.

*Improv Topic:*
- Trust
- Spontaneity
- Accepting offers
- Listening and awareness
- Storytelling
- Nonverbal behavior

*Purpose:*
- Team building
- Creativity
- Communication
- Problem solving

*Supplies:*
- None

*Time:*
- 2–3 minutes per round

*Number of Players:*
- Pairs

*Game Flow:*
- In each pair assign a person A and person B.
- Person B plays the role of someone from 300 years ago.
- Person A endeavors to explain a modern-day object (e.g., a cell phone, a television, an airplane, a microwave oven) to person B.
- Partners switch roles and repeat.

*Variations:*
- Tell the As the object secretly, without the Bs knowing.

- Add a round in which pairs explain to each other some technical process or skill or area of knowledge that they are expert in, but their partner is not familiar with.

*Tips:*
- Encourage person B to wholeheartedly embrace the character and mind-set of someone from 300 years ago. (Hint: Lots of different things were happening in different parts of the world, but electricity was not in use yet.)
- Perhaps demo the activity, playing person B. Illustrate misunder-standing of non-period words, for example: "Wait, you press a button? Like on my shirt?"

*Suggested Debrief Questions:*
- How did you approach your task at first?
- What strategies did you use?
- What was it like to take on the mind-set of someone from 300 years ago?
- What judgments did you make or not make about the inability of the person from 300 years ago to understand the object?
- What is this like in real life? What gaps do you need to navigate?
- How can thinking of those gaps like you thought of this gap help you be a more effective communicator?

*Source:*
- Performance of a Lifetime.

# Billy, Billy, Bop

*Overview:*
- A circle game in which one person is "It." She stands in the center, saying a series of cues. If she catches someone making a mistake in responding, that person takes her place in the center.

*Improv Topic:*
- Trust
- Spontaneity
- Listening and awareness

*Purpose:*
- Icebreaker
- Team building
- Creativity
- Communication
- Energy builder
- Warm-up

*Supplies:*
- None

*Time:*
- 10–15 minutes

*Number of Players:*
- 5–20

*Game Flow:*
- Participants stand in a circle with one person in the middle.
- Middle person faces one of the others and says either:
  - "Billy, Billy, Bop" or
  - "Bop"
- If the middle person says "Billy, Billy, Bop," the partner must say "Bop" before the middle person finishes.
- If the middle person says, "Bop," the partner must be silent.
- After a few rounds, other cues may be added:
  - The middle person may shout a word that is associated with a gesture. Then they count out loud to 10.

- If the people in the circle do not hit the correct pose before the middle person gets to 10, they are in the middle.
- Poses include:
  - "Bunny"—chosen player makes paws; players on either side make ears on either side of the center player's head.
  - "Charlie's Angels"—chosen player and those on either side make some version of the old Charlie's Angels pose with guns bared.
  - "Orchestra"—chosen player plays a cello; player on her right plays a flute; player on her left plays a violin.

*Variations:*
- Add a "caller's choice" option in which the player in the middle can say any word, and the three players chosen must form some kind of tableau.
- Play as an elimination game until there are only five players left.

*Tips:*
- Success at the game depends on paying attention more than anything else. Remind players that focus is a muscle that can be exercised.
- The game offers an opportunity for players to fail good-naturedly. Perhaps teach the Circus Bow first (see "I Failed!").
- Encourage the group to go fast.
- Start as the first player in the center.

*Suggested Debrief Questions:*
*(N.B.: as a warm-up game or energizer, you may find no extensive debrief necessary.)*
- What strategies did you employ?
- What made this fun? Not fun?
- When were you most focused? Distracted?

*Source:*
- BATS Improv, Theatresports community.

# Gesture Pass

*Overview:*
- In a circle, participants create unique gestures that they pass around the circle. A variation of "Slap Pass" (see page 197).

*Improv Topic:*
- Trust
- Spontaneity
- Accepting offers
- Listening and awareness
- Nonverbal communication

*Purpose:*
- Icebreaker
- Team building
- Creativity
- Communication
- Energy builder
- Warm-up

*Supplies:*
- None

*Time:*
- 5–15 minutes

*Number of Players:*
- 6–20 ideally

*Game Flow:*
- Participants stand in a circle.
- The first two participants (A and B) face each other and find a gesture and sound together by mirroring each other.
- Then B turns to C, and they find another sound and gesture. C turns to D, and so on around the circle.
- Once the gestures are established, the energy/gestures make their way around the circle, each pair performing their unique gesture when the "energy" comes to them.

- If a person wishes to switch the direction of the energy they remain facing their last partner and repeat the gesture to send it back the way it came from.

*Variations:*
- Give everyone the same word to start.
- Play more than once with different partners.
- Play for two minutes, seeing how many times the partners can say the same word.

*Tips:*
- Coach the pairs to say their words with great energy and enthusiasm.
- Coach the pairs to celebrate and cheer when they succeed.
- Remind people that the task is impossible, and they should not get discouraged if they do not succeed.

*Suggested Debrief Questions:*
*(N.B.: This may be a fun icebreaker/energizer without the need for a long debrief.)*
- Did you succeed?
- How did it feel to succeed?
- What if you did not? How did that feel?
- Why were you able to succeed?
- How does connecting this way with someone else feel?
- How is your energy now, individually and collectively?

*Source:*
- The PIT, Dion Flynn.

# Metaphor Builder

*Overview:*
- A process for creating and building metaphors. Useful for making presentations more vivid and deepening understanding and retention.

*Improv Topic:*
- Spontaneity
- Accepting offers
- Storytelling

*Purpose:*
- Team building
- Creativity
- Communication
- Problem solving

*Supplies:*
- Paper and pens
- Flip charts, if desired

*Time:*
- 10–15 minutes

*Number of Players:*
- 1–8 per group

*Game Flow:*
- Choose a process or product.
- Step 1: Brainstorm qualities of that product or process.
- Step 2: Brainstorm other things that share those qualities.
- Step 3: Each group picks one of the brainstormed objects and extends the metaphor, finding additional similarities between the original product or process and then object.
- Groups present: "A _____ is like a _____, because. . . ."

*Variations:*
- Play as a spontaneity game in a circle, each person getting two unrelated objects and saying, "A _____ is like a _____,

because. . . ." So, A says "popcorn," B says "sea lion," and person C says, "Popcorn is like a sea lion, because they both delight children." Then B says "candle," and C says "taxes," and D says "A candle is like taxes, because they can both keep you working late into the night." And so on. (This is a good version to play as a warm-up to the more content-driven activity previously outlined.)

- Start with a problem and assign random objects. Then each group says, "The solution to this problem is like a _____" and explains their solution.

*Tips:*
- Remind the groups not to censor or evaluate during brainstorming sessions.
- The "Metaphor Builder" game is about expanding our ways of thinking; this process is as useful as the actual content generated. Feel free to debrief both separately.
- You may wish to do various rounds, some individually, some in pairs, some in larger groups.

*Suggested Debrief Questions:*
- How was that process?
- What became clearer about the nature of your product, process, or problem?
- When and how might using this metaphor help?
- What is the value of using metaphor in general?

*Source:*
- Koppett + Company, LLC Storytelling for Leaders.

# The Observation Game

*Overview:*
- In pairs, participants observe each other's behavior, creating a scene simply by naming their partner's physical offers.

*Improv Topic:*
- Trust
- Spontaneity
- Accepting offers
- Listening and awareness
- Nonverbal behavior

*Purpose:*
- Team building
- Creativity
- Communication
- Energy builder
- Warm-up

*Supplies:*
- None

*Time:*
- 5–15 minutes

*Number of Players:*
- Pairs

*Game Flow:*
- Pairs of participants face each other in neutral position.
- Person A looks at her partner and names something they are doing: e.g., "I see you raise your eyebrows."
- Then person A continues, "And I _____."
- Person B responds, "I see you ____, and I _____."
- The exercise continues with each person observing the other and naming what they see and their response.

*Variations:*
- Use as a demonstration game with two volunteers.

- Have players start by naming their own action.
- Change the phrases to:
  - "I see you _____, which makes me feel/want _____. So I _____."
- Advanced: Offer participants a scenario, and have them play the game in character. For example:
  - A job interview.
  - Giving feedback.
  - A sales call.
  - A first date.

*Tips:*
- Coach participants to dare to be boring or obvious.
- Remind participants to pay attention to as many different kinds of offers as possible.
- Start with a demonstration.

*Suggested Debrief Questions:*
- How did it feel to pay attention in that way?
- How did it feel to be paid attention to like that?
- What judgments did you find yourself making?
- How many different kinds of offers were you able to recognize?
- How could paying attention in this way apply to real life?

*Source:*
- Michael Burns, The Mop & Bucket Company.

# Read My Mind

*Overview:*
- In pairs, participants simultaneously shout out words that come to mind, free-associating off of the last words that were said, until both people shout out the same word at the same time.

*Improv Topic:*
- Trust
- Spontaneity
- Accepting offers
- Listening and awareness

*Purpose:*
- Team building
- Creativity
- Communication
- Energy builder
- Warm-up

*Supplies:*
- None

*Time:*
- 1 minute per round

*Number of Players:*
- Pairs

*Game Flow:*
- Participants face each other in pairs.
- Simultaneously they shout out whatever random word comes to mind. (They can do it on a count of three if they like.)
- The process continues, participants free-associating based on previous words, until both people shout the same word at the same time.
- Start again.

*Variations:*
- Give everyone the same word to start.

- Play more than once with different partners.
- Play for two minutes seeing how many times the partners can say the same word.

*Tips:*
- Coach the pairs to say their words with great energy and enthusiasm.
- Coach the pairs to celebrate and cheer when they succeed.
- Remind people that the task is impossible, and they should not get discouraged if they do not succeed.

*Suggested Debrief Questions:*
*(N.B.: This may be a fun icebreaker/engergizer without the need for a long debrief.)*
- Did you succeed?
- How did it feel to succeed?
- What if you did not? How did that feel?
- Why were you able to succeed?
- How does connecting this way with someone else feel?
- How is your energy now, individually and collectively?

*Source:*
- BATS Improv, Chris Sams.

# Rope!

*Overview:*
- A scenic game in which one person starts a physical action, another initiates an unrelated line of dialogue, and the first person must justify both. If the audience is not satisfied with the justification, it yells, "Rope!" and the team must try again from the beginning with a new activity and line.

*Improv Topic:*
- Spontaneity
- Accepting offers
- Listening and awareness
- Nonverbal behavior

*Purpose:*
- Team building
- Creativity
- Communication
- Energy builder
- Warm-up

*Supplies:*
- None

*Time:*
- 1 minute per round

*Number of Players:*
- Pairs

*Game Flow:*
- Participant 1 starts a physical action (e.g., washing dishes).
- Particpant 2, without looking, thinks of an opening line of dialogue for a scene.
- When cued, participant 2 enters and says her line of dialogue.
- Participant 1 must respond in a way that both "yes, ands" the first line and justifies his action.
- If the audience is unsatisfied with the justification, people yell "Rope!," and the pair will try again.

- When participant 1 succeeds, he leaves; participant 2 takes his place and starts an action. Participant 3 enters with a line of dialogue, and so on.

*Variations:*
- Play round-robin without shouting "rope," allowing each person to simply succeed to the best of their ability.

*Tips:*
- Coach the audience to shout "rope" with enthusiasm. The failure should be acknowledged and perfectly okay.
- Remind the participants to "dare to be obvious." The simpler justifications are often the most satisfying.

*Suggested Debrief Questions:*
- How did you come up with your activities/lines of dialogue?
- How easy/hard was it to justify?
- What ideas, if any, did you block?
- How did it feel from an audience perspective when the justification was successful?
- How did it feel to yell "rope"? What is the value of practicing shouting and receiving a "rope"?

*Source:*
- The Mop & Bucket Company, Michael Burns.

# String of Pearls Storytelling

*Overview:*
- One sentence at a time, participants create a story, adding their sentences in random order, building the story as they go.

*Improv Topic:*
- Accepting offers
- Listening and awareness
- Storytelling

*Purpose:*
- Team building
- Creativity
- Communication
- Review
- Problem solving
- Closing

*Supplies:*
- None

*Time:*
- 5–6 minutes per round

*Number of Players:*
- 7–10 per round

*Game Flow:*
- One person steps on stage and offers a sentence that could belong "somewhere near the beginning of a story."
- The next person stands at the other end of the stage and adds another sentence that they believe belongs "somewhere near the end."
- 5–7 more people add sentences to complete the story, standing closer to person 1 or 2, depending on where they believe their sentence should go.
- After each sentence, the whole story is repeated in order, until all the participants are used and the story is complete.
  Example:
  Sentence #1—"Joe loved fishing."
  Sentence #2—"And they never went to the lake again."
  Sentence #3—(added close to sentence one) "But this time, what he pulled up on the end of his hook wasn't a fish . . ."

Sentence #4—(added in between sentence #1 and sentence #3) "Every day he went down to the lake and caught fish for his dinner." Sentence #5—(added close to sentence #2) "Finally Joe and the mermaid killed the octopus monster!"
So the story at this point would read:
Joe loved fishing. Every day he went down to the lake and caught fish for his dinner. But this time, what he pulled up on the end of his hook wasn't a fish. . . . Finally, Joe and the mermaid killed the octopus monster. . . . And they never went to the lake again. Subsequent players would fill in the remaining gaps.

*Variations:*
- Ask the participants to explain a business process.
- Ask the participants to recount a real-life event they experienced together.
- Do a couple of rounds telling sentence-at-a-time stories in order first.
- Use the Story Spine as a template, asking participants to start their sentence with one of those cue phrases.

*Tips:*
- Encourage the second person to add a sentence really remote from the first. If he is not sure what the connection might be, that's fine.
- Remind the participants to repeat the story as it stands so far, each time a new sentence is added.
- If participants hesitate, coach them to add one small detail or bit of action. Tell them to figure out what questions they have as an audience and make a choice to answer one of them.

*Suggested Debrief Questions:*
- How did that feel?
- What moments were most satisfying?
- How did you choose what to add?
- How does a good sense of what is needed narratively help us?
- How is this activity like your work tasks?

*Source:*
- Freestyle Repertory Theatre, Theatresports community.

# Superheroes

*Overview:*
- A circle game in which each person creates a superhero identity and a gesture to go with it. Once the gestures are created, players call and respond to gestures.

*Improv Topic:*
- Trust
- Spontaneity
- Accepting offers
- Listening and awareness
- Nonverbal behavior

*Purpose:*
- Icebreaker
- Team building
- Creativity
- Communication
- Energy builder
- Warm-up

*Supplies:*
- None

*Time:*
- 10–15 minutes

*Number of Players:*
- 5–20

*Game Flow:*
- Participants stand in a circle. Each takes a turn creating a superhero name and gesture (e.g., Multi-Tasking Man, The Organizer, Coffee Boy, Late-for-Work Woman).
- As each person creates their name and gesture, the group repeats it to learn it.
- Then, the group goes around the circle one more time, in unison, learning others' gestures.

- Once the gestures are established and learned, one player starts, saying his name with his gesture. Then he says someone else's name while doing their gesture.
- That person then does their own name and gesture and someone else's. And so on.

*Variations:*
- See how fast the players can go.
- Call and respond as if the name is a secret.
- Call and respond as if _____ (e.g., you are a preacher, you are a small child, you are the queen).

*Tips:*
- The faster they go, the more fun they'll have.
- Coach the players to commit and be large.
- Superheroes can be ANYTHING!

*Suggested Debrief Questions:*
*(N.B.: As a warm-up game or energizer, you may find no extensive debrief necessary.)*
- How did you choose your hero?
- What made this fun? Not fun?
- When were you most focused? Distracted?
- How do you feel now, compared with before we started?

*Source:*
- Chicago Improv schools.

APPENDIX

# ACTIVITIES/IMPROV TOPICS

| ACTIVITY | TRUST | SPONTANEITY | ACCEPTING OFFERS | LISTENING & AWARENESS | STORYTELLING | NONVERBAL BEHAVIOR |
|---|---|---|---|---|---|---|
| Accept This! | | X | X | | | |
| Ask a Silly Question | X | X | X | | | |
| Awareness Quiz | | | | X | | |
| Ball Ball | X | | X | X | | |
| Ball Toss | X | | X | X | | |
| Blindfold Walk | X | | | X | | X |
| But Versus And | | | X | X | | |
| Character Creation | X | X | X | X | X | X |
| Circle Mirror | X | | | X | | X |
| Classic Mirror | X | | | X | | X |
| Color/Advance | | X | X | X | X | |
| Conducted Narrative | | X | X | X | X | |
| Conversation Weave | | | X | X | X | |
| Declare Yourself | X | | | X | | X |
| Elimination Lists | X | X | | X | | |

| Activity | Trust | Spontaneity | Accepting Offers | Listening & Awareness | Storytelling | Nonverbal Behavior |
|---|---|---|---|---|---|---|
| Emotional Meeting | X | X | X | X | | X |
| Expert Interviews | X | X | X | X | X | X |
| Gibberish Press Conference | | X | X | | X | X |
| Giving Gifts | X | X | X | | | X |
| Group Counting | X | | | X | | |
| Hum Circle | X | X | X | X | | |
| I Failed! | X | X | | | | |
| Idea Circle | | X | | | | |
| Invisible Balls | X | X | X | X | | X |
| Neutral Status Scene | | | | X | X | X |
| One-Sided Scene | | | X | X | | X |
| One-Word-at-a-Time Exercises | | X | X | X | X | |
| Paired Drawing | | X | X | | | X |
| Picture Math | | X | X | X | X | |
| Picture Poetry | | X | X | X | X | |
| Safety Zone | | X | X | X | X | X |

(continues)

| Activity | Trust | Spontaneity | Accepting Offers | Listening & Awareness | Storytelling | Nonverbal Behavior |
|---|---|---|---|---|---|---|
| Slap Pass | X | X | X | X | X | X |
| Speaking in Unison | | X | X | X | X | |
| Speech Tag | | X | X | X | X | X |
| Spontaneous Marketing | | X | X | | | |
| Stats | X | X | | | | |
| Status Cards | | | | X | | X |
| Status Demo | X | | | X | | X |
| Status Pass | X | | | | | X |
| Story Exchange | X | | X | X | X | X |
| Story of Your Name | X | | | | X | |
| Story Seeds | | | X | | X | |
| The Story Spine Story | | X | X | X | X | |
| Story Visioning | X | | X | | X | |
| True or False | | | X | X | X | X |
| Vision Weaving | X | X | X | X | X | |

| Activity | Trust | Spontaneity | Accepting Offers | Listening & Awareness | Storytelling | Nonverbal Behavior |
|---|---|---|---|---|---|---|
| Warm-up: Physical and Vocal | | X | | X | | X |
| Word Drill | X | X | X | | | |
| Word Patterns | X | | X | X | | |
| You're Out | X | | X | X | X | X |
| Three Things in Common | X | X | | X | | X |
| The 300-Year Gap Conversation | X | X | X | X | X | |
| Billy, Billy, Bop | X | X | | X | | |
| Gesture Pass | X | X | X | X | | X |
| Metaphor Builder | | X | X | | X | |
| The Observation Game | X | X | X | X | | X |
| Read My Mind | X | X | X | X | | |
| Rope! | | X | X | X | | X |
| String of Pearls Storytelling | | | X | X | X | |
| Superheroes | X | X | X | X | | X |

# ACTIVITIES/TRAINING USES

| Activity | Supplies | Time | # of Players | Ice-breaker | Team Building | Crea-tivity | Commun-ication | Review | Needs Assess. | Problem Solving | Energy Builder | Warm-up | Closing |
|---|---|---|---|---|---|---|---|---|---|---|---|---|---|
| Accept This! | None | 8–15 minutes | Pairs | | X | X | X | | | | X | X | |
| Ask a Silly Question | None | 3–8 minutes | Various | | X | X | X | | | | X | X | |
| Awareness Quiz | None | 3–5 minutes | Pairs | | X | X | X | | | | X | X | |
| Ball Ball | None | 7–15 minutes | 4–20 | X | X | | X | X | X | | X | X | X |
| Ball Toss | 5–10 soft juggling balls or sacks | 10–30 minutes | 6–20 | X | X | | X | | | | X | X | X |
| Blindfold Walk | None | 10–20 minutes | Pairs | | X | | X | | | | | X | |
| But Versus And | None | 4–8 minutes | Various | | X | X | X | | | | | | |
| Character Creation | None | 10–20 minutes | 2–20 | | X | X | X | | | | | X | |
| Circle Mirror | None | 5–7 minutes | 6–20 | | X | X | X | | | | X | | |
| Classic Mirror | None | 8–15 minutes | Pairs | | X | | X | | | | | X | |
| Color/Advance | A flip chart, slide, or handout with the Story Spine recorded | 5–15 minutes | Pairs | | | X | X | X | X | X | | | |
| Conducted Narrative | None | 3–6 minutes | 4–5 per round | | X | X | X | X | | | | X | |

| Activity | Supplies | Time | # of Players | Ice-breaker | Team Building | Creativity | Communication | Review | Needs Assess. | Problem Solving | Energy Builder | Warm-up | Closing |
|---|---|---|---|---|---|---|---|---|---|---|---|---|---|
| Conversation Weave | None | 8–15 minutes per group | 3–4 per group | | X | X | X | | | | | | |
| Declare Yourself | None | 5–15 minutes | 3–20 | X | X | | X | X | X | | | X | X |
| Elimination Lists | None | 6–12 minutes | 4–20, plus observers | X | X | X | X | X | | | X | X | |
| Emotional Meeting | Chairs and table (optional) Flipchart (optional) | 5–10 minutes per group | 3–5 per group | | X | | X | | | | X | | |
| Expert Interviews | Two chairs | 7–15 minutes per group | Pairs | | X | X | X | X | X | X | | | |
| Gibberish Press Conference | None | 5–30 minutes | Pairs | | X | X | X | X | | | X | | |
| Giving Gifts | None | 5–15 minutes | Pairs | X | X | X | X | | | | | X | |
| Group Counting | None | 3–10 minutes | 4–20 | | X | | X | | | | | | X |
| Hum Circle | None | 5–10 minutes | 4–16 | | X | | X | | | | | X | X |
| I Failed! | None | 2–5 minutes | 2–1,000 | X | X | X | X | | | X | X | X | |
| Idea Circle | One object | 20–30 seconds per participant per round | 10–20 | | | X | | X | | | X | X | |

(continues)

| Activity | Supplies | Time | # of Players | Ice-breaker | Team Building | Crea-tivity | Commun-ication | Review | Needs Assess. | Problem Solving | Energy Builder | Warm-up | Closing |
|---|---|---|---|---|---|---|---|---|---|---|---|---|---|
| Invisible Balls | None | 5–20 minutes | 4–20 per group | X | X | X | X | | | | X | X | |
| Neutral Status Scene | Handouts, flip chart or slide with the scene recorded | 15–30 minutes | Pairs | | X | | X | | | | | | |
| One-Sided Scene | None | 3–5 minutes per role play | Pairs | | X | | X | | | | | | |
| One-Word-at-a-Time Exercises | None | 5–30 minutes | 2–20 | | X | X | X | X | | | X | X | |
| Paired Drawing | Colored pens and paper, flip charts | 10–20 minutes | Pairs | | X | X | X | | | | | | |
| Picture Math | None | 10–15 minutes | Trios | | | X | | | | | X | X | |
| Picture Poetry | None | 4–10 minutes | Pairs | | X | X | X | | | | | X | |
| Safety Zone | None | 3–6 minutes | 8–100 | | X | | | | | | X | X | |
| Slap Pass | None | 5–15 minutes | 5–25 | | X | X | X | | | | X | X | |
| Speaking in Unison | None | 3–5 minutes per group | 3–5 per group | | X | X | X | X | | | X | X | |
| Speech Tag | None | 3–5 minutes | 3–5 per group | | X | X | X | X | | | | | |

| Activity | Supplies | Time | # of Players | Ice-breaker | Team building | Creativity | Communication | Review | Needs Assess. | Problem Solving | Energy Builder | Warm-up | Closing |
|---|---|---|---|---|---|---|---|---|---|---|---|---|---|
| Spontaneous Marketing | Flip charts (1 per group) Markers | 15–20 minutes plus 3 minutes per group to share | 2–5 per group | X | X | X | X | | | | | | |
| Stats | One chair per participant | 15–30 minutes | 6–20 per circle | X | X | | X | | X | | X | X | |
| Status Cards | 1 playing card per person | 10–20 minutes | 5–100 | | X | | X | | | | X | X | |
| Status Demo | None | 5–15 minutes | 5–100 | | X | | X | | | | | X | |
| Status Pass | None | 5–15 minutes | 2–20 per group | | X | | X | | | | | X | |
| Story Exchange | 3"x5" cards Pens | 25–50 minutes | 10–20 | X | X | X | X | | | | | | |
| Story of Your Name | None | 1–2 minutes per participant | Variable | X | X | | X | | | | | X | |
| Story Seeds | Pens and paper | 10–20 minutes | Variable | | | X | X | X | X | X | | | |
| Story Visioning | A flip chart and pens | 30–60 minutes | 2–20 | | X | X | X | | X | X | | | |
| The Story Spine Story | A flip chart, slide, or handout with the Story Spine recorded | 10–60 minutes | 1–5 per group | | X | X | X | X | X | X | | X | X |

(continues)

| ACTIVITY | SUPPLIES | TIME | # OF PLAYERS | ICE-BREAKER | TEAM BUILDING | CREA-TIVITY | COMMUN-ICATION | REVIEW | NEEDS ASSESS. | PROBLEM SOLVING | ENERGY BUILDER | WARM-UP | CLOSING |
|---|---|---|---|---|---|---|---|---|---|---|---|---|---|
| True or False | None | 15 minute preparation (or prep assigned ahead of time) plus 10 minutes per participant | Variable | | X | X | X | | | | | | |
| Vision Weaving | A flip chart and pens or a tape recorder | 10–20 minutes | 2–20 | | X | X | X | | X | X | | X | X |
| Warm-up: Physical and Vocal | None | 7–10 minutes | 1–200 | X | | | X | | | | X | X | |
| Word Drill | None | 6–12 minutes | 3–5 per group | | | X | X | | | | X | X | |
| Word Patterns | None | 15–20 minutes | 6–20 | X | X | | X | | | | X | X | |
| You're Out | None | 3–5 minutes per scene | 3 per scene | | X | | X | | | | | | |

# ADDITIONAL ACTIVITIES

| Activity | Supplies | Time | # of Players | Ice-breaker | Team building | Crea-tivity | Commun-ication | Review | Needs Assess. | Problem Solving | Energy Builder | Warm-up | Closing |
|---|---|---|---|---|---|---|---|---|---|---|---|---|---|
| Three Things in Common | None | 2–3 minutes per round | Pairs | X | X | X | X |  | X |  | X | X |  |
| The 300-Year-Gap Conversation | None | 2–3 minutes per round | Pairs |  | X | X | X |  |  | X |  |  |  |
| Billy, Billy, Bop | None | 10–15 minutes | 5–20 | X | X | X | X |  |  |  | X | X |  |
| Gesture Pass | None | 5–15 minutes | 6–20 | X | X | X | X |  |  |  | X | X |  |
| Metaphor Builder | Paper, pens, flip chart | 10–15 minutes | 1–8 per group |  | X | X | X | X |  | X |  |  |  |
| The Observation Game | None | 5–15 minutes | Pairs |  | X | X | X |  |  |  | X | X |  |
| Read My Mind | None | 1 minute per round | Pairs |  | X | X | X |  |  |  | X | X |  |
| Rope! | None | 1 minute per round | Pairs |  | X | X | X |  |  |  | X | X |  |
| String of Pearls Storytelling | None | 5–6 minutes per round | 7–10 |  | X | X | X | X |  | X |  |  | X |
| Superheroes | None | 10–15 minutes | 5–20 | X | X | X | X |  |  |  | X | X |  |

## Introduction

1. Johnstone, K. (1979). *Impro: Improvisation and the theatre*. New York, NY: Theatre Arts Books.
2. Halpern, C., Close, D., & Johnson, K. (1994). *Truth in comedy: The manual of improvisation*. Colorado Springs, CO: Meriwether Publishing, LTD.
3. Spolin, V. (1983). *Improvisation for the theater*. Evanston, IL: Northwestern University.

## Chapter 1

4. Spolin, V. (1983).
5. Halpern, C., Close, D., & Johnson, K. (1994).
6. Mehrabian, A. (1971). *Silent messages*. Belmont, CA: Wadsworth.
7. Johnstone, K. (1979).

## Chapter 2

8. MacKenzie, G. (1996). *Orbiting the giant hairball: A corporate fool's guide to surviving with grace*. New York, NY: Viking.

## Chapter 3

9. Spolin, V. (1983).
10. Lamott, A. (1994). *Bird by bird*. New York, NY: Anchor Books.
11. Johnstone, K. (1979).
12. Richter, M. (2001). Creating intrinsically motivating environments: A motivation system. In S. Thiagarajan (Ed.) *ASTD Interventions*. ASTD.
13. Johnstone, K. (1979).
14. MacKenzie, G. (1996).
15. Suzuki, S. (1985). *Zen mind, beginner's mind: Informal talks on Zen meditation and practice*. New York, NY: Weatherhill.
16. Blatner, A., & Blatner, A. (1997). *The art of play: Helping adults reclaim imagination and spontaneity* (Rev. ed.). New York, NY: Brunner/Mazel.

## Chapter 4

17. Halpern, C., Close, D., & Johnson, K. (1994).
18. Spolin, V. (1983).
19. Johnstone, K. (1979).
20. Seligman, M. E. P. (1998). *Learned optimism: How to change your mind and your life*. New York, NY: Pocket Books.
21. Seligman, M. E. P. (1998).
22. Johnstone, K. (1979).

23. Johnstone, K. (1979).
24. Richter, M. (2001).

## Chapter 7

25. Chekhov, M. (1953). *To the actor: On the technique of acting.* New York, NY: Harper and Row.
26. Parkin, M. (1998). *Tales for trainers: Using stories and metaphors to facilitate learning.* London: Kogan Page Limited.
27. Johnstone, K. (1979).
28. Johnstone, K. (1979).
29. Allred, K. (1996). *Class notes, Negotiation.* New York, NY: Columbia University.
30. Johnstone, K. (1979).
31. French, J. R. P., & Raven, B. H. (1959). The bases of social power. In D. Cartwright (Ed.), *Studies in social power.* Ann Arbor, MI: Institute for Social Research.

Adams, K. (2007). *How to improvise a full-length play: The art of spontaneous theater.* New York, NY: Allworth Press.

Allred, K. (1996). *Class notes, Negotiation.* New York, NY: Columbia University.

Argyris, C. (1990). *Overcoming organizational defenses: Facilitating organizational learning.* Boston, MA: Allyn and Bacon.

Armstrong, D. (1992). *Managing by storying around: A new method of leadership.* New York, NY: Doubleday.

Badaracco, J. L. (1997). *Defining moments: When managers must choose between right and right.* Boston, MA: Harvard Business School Press.

Bal, M. (1985). *Narratology: Introduction to the theory of narrative.* Buffalo, NY: University of Toronto Press.

Belt, L., & Stockley, R. (1991). *Improvisation through TheatreSports: A curriculum to improve acting skills.* Seattle, WA: Thespis Productions.

Blatner, A., & Blatner, A. (1997). *The art of play: Helping adults reclaim imagination and spontaneity* (Rev. ed.). New York, NY: Brunner/Mazel.

Bruner, J. (1990). *Acts of meaning.* Cambridge, MA: Harvard University Press.

Burns, J. M. (1978). *Leadership.* New York, NY: Harper Torchbooks.

Cameron, J. (1992). *The artist's way: A spiritual path to higher creativity.* Los Angeles, CA: Jeremy P. Tarcher/Perigee.

Campbell, J. (1973). *The hero with a thousand faces.* Princeton, NJ: Bollingen Series/ Princeton University Press.

Chabris, C., & Simon, D. (2010). *The invisible gorilla: And other ways our intuitions deceive us.* New York, NY: Crown.

Chekhov, M. (1953). *To the actor: On the technique of acting.* New York, NY: Harper and Row.

Deci, E. L., & Flaste, R. (1996). *Why we do what we do: Understanding self-motivation.* New York, NY: Penguin.

Denning, S. (2001). *The springboard: How storytelling ignites action in knowledge-era organizations.* Boston, MA: Butterworth-Heinemann.

Fisher, R., Ury, W., & Patton, B. (1991). *Getting to yes: Negotiating agreement without giving in.* New York, NY: Penguin Books.

French, J. R. P., & Raven, B. H. (1959). The bases of social power. In D. Cartwright (Ed.), *Studies in social power.* Ann Arbor, MI: Institute for Social Research.

Godin, S. *The flip side.* Retrieved April 28, 2011, from http://sethgodin.typepad.com/ seths_blog/2011/04/the-flip-side.html (page 34).

Goleman, D. (1996). *Emotional intelligence: Why it can matter more than IQ.* London: Bloomsbury.

Goleman, D. (1998). *Working with emotional intelligence.* New York, NY: Bantam Books.

Hall, D., & Wecker, D. (1995). *Jump start your brain.* New York, NY: Warner Books.

Halpern, C., Close, D., & Johnson, K. (1994). *Truth in comedy: The manual of improvisation.* Colorado Springs, CO: Meriwether Publishing, LTD.

Horrey, W., & Wickens, C. (2006). Examining the impact of cell phone conversations on driving using meta-analytic techniques. *Human Factors (Human Factors and Ergonomics Society)*, 38(1), 196–205.

Iyengar, S. (2010). *Sheena Iyengar: The art of choosing.* (Video file). Retrieved from http://www.ted.com/talks/sheena_iyengar_on_the_art_of_choosing.html

Johnstone, K. (1979). *Impro: Improvisation and the theatre.* New York, NY: Theatre Arts Books.

Johnstone, K. (1999). *Impro for storytellers.* New York, NY: Theatre Arts Books.

Jones, C., & O'Brien, J. (1991). *Mistakes that worked.* New York, NY: Doubleday.

Lamott, A. (1994). *Bird by bird.* New York, NY: Anchor Books.

Lee, H. (1960). *To kill a mockingbird.* Philadelphia, PA: Lippincott.

Leman, K. (1996). *Winning the rat race without becoming a rat.* Nashville, TN: Nelson.

Levine, J., & Moreland, R. (2002). Socialization and trust in work groups: Group process and intergroup relations 5(3). *Group Processes Intergroup Relations,* 185–201.

Lewis, T., & Nichols, R. (1964). *Speaking and listening: A guide to effective oral-aural communication.* Dubuque, IA: Brown Co.

MacKenzie, G. (1996). *Orbiting the giant hairball: A corporate fool's guide to surviving with grace.* New York, NY: Viking.

Mehrabian, A. (1971). *Silent messages.* Belmont, CA: Wadsworth.

Mellon, N. (1992). *The art of storytelling.* Boston, MA: Element.

Neirenberg, G., & Calero, H. (1971). *How to read a person like a book.* New York, NY: Hawthorn Books.

Parkin, M. (1998). *Tales for trainers: Using stories and metaphors to facilitate learning.* London: Kogan Page Limited.

Pink, Daniel. (2006). *A whole new mind: Why right-brainers will rule the future.* New York, NY: Riverhead Books.

Ray, M. (2008). *Creativity in business.* DVD, Kantola Productions, Mill Valley, CA.

Richter, M. (2001) Creating intrinsically motivating environments: A motivation system. In S. Thiagarajan (Ed.), (n.p.) *ASTD Interventions.* ASTD.

Schank, R. (1995). *Tell me a story: Narrative and intelligence.* Evanston, IL: Northwestern University.

Seligman, M. E. P. (1998). *Learned optimism: How to change your mind and your life.* New York, NY: Pocket Books.

Sen, A. (1999). *Development as freedom.* New York, NY: Alfred A. Knopf.

Senge, P. M. (1990). *The fifth discipline: The art & practice of the learning organization.* New York, NY: Doubleday.

Shakespeare, W., & Hosley, R. (1954). *The tragedy of Romeo and Juliet.* New Haven, CT: Yale University Press.

Simmons, A., & Lipman, D. (2006). *The story factor: Secrets of influence from the art of storytelling.* New York, NY: Basic Books.

Spolin, V. (1983). *Improvisation for the theater.* Evanston, IL: Northwestern University.

Suzuki, S. (1985). *Zen mind, beginner's mind: Informal talks on Zen meditation and practice.* New York, NY: Weatherhill.

Tavris, S., & Aronson, E. (2007). *Mistakes were made (but not by me): Why we justify foolish beliefs, bad decisions, and hurtful acts.* Orlando, FL: Harcourt.

Thiagarajan, S., & Thiagarajan, R. (2000). *Interactive strategies for improving performance: 10 powerful tools.* Bloomington, IN: Workshops by Thiagi.

Thiagi Group. (2004). "Seriously fun activities for trainers, facilitators, performance consultants, and managers." *Play for Performance.* Retrieved from: http://www.thiagi.com/pfp/IE4H/february2004.html.

Ury, W. (2007). *The power of a positive no: How to say no and still get to yes.* New York, NY: Bantam Books.

Vogler, C. (1998). *The writer's journey: Mythic structure for writers.* Studio City, CA: Michael Wiese Productions.

Vroom, V. H., & Deci, E. L. (Eds.) (1992). *Management and motivation.* New York, NY: Penguin Books.

Wiesel, E. (1966). *The gates of the forest.* New York, NY: Holt, Rinehart and Winston.

# KOPPETT + COMPANY

WEAVING PASSION INTO PERFORMANCE

Koppett + Company (Kopco) is a consulting and training company focused on enhancing individual and group performance through the application of theatre, story, and improvisational principles. Kopco consultants have unique, blended backgrounds in the areas of organizational development, instructional design, acting, playwriting, and directing, allowing them to create cross-disciplinary programs that develop leadership, creativity, and presentation skills. We have been called "thought-leaders" in the field of Applied Improv, and pride themselves on building rigorous, outcome-focused programs, even when coaching the softest of soft skills.

We have designed and delivered programs for a diverse, global list of clients including Fortune 100 companies, non-profits, educational institutions, small businesses, and government agencies.

Our sister company, The Mop & Bucket Company (Mopco), is a professional improvisational theatre that brings performance skills to audiences of all kinds, including corporate events, private parties, public performances, and video projects.

For more information go to www.koppett.com or call 518-847-9882.